15.

First edition published in Thailand by River Books 1995
and distributed in the UK by New Cavendish Books
3 Denbigh Road, London W11 2SJ
tel: 0171 229 6765
fax: 0171 792 0027

Design and typesetting by Supadee Ruangsak
Illustrated by Gee Thomson
Publisher and Editor Narisa Chakra
Production by Paisarn Piemmettawat

Printed and bound in Thailand by Namaksorn Printing
ISBN 974 8363 47 3

CONTENTS

Foreword	5	*Chapter 10* Aspects of Consciousness	73
Prologue	6	*Chapter 11* A Test of Astrology	79
Chapter 1 The Satipatthāna Sutta	9	*Chapter 12* Do You Believe in Belief?	83
Chapter 2 What the Buddha taught the Kālāmas	15	*Chapter 13* Form is Emptiness and Emptiness Form	87
Chapter 3 Essential Buddhism	17	*Chapter 14* The Karma Buck Stops Here	91
Chapter 4 Sāti the Fisherman's Son	23	*Chapter 15* The World a Dream?	95
Chapter 5 Buddhism and Science	31	*Chapter 16* The Perennial Practice	101
Chapter 6 Involvement	43	Epilogue	105
Chapter 7 Busier than Ever!	49	Glossary	106
Chapter 8 The Honey-Cake	53	Notes and References	113
Chapter 9 The Story of Māgandiya's Conversion	63	Index	123

To the wisdom and compassion latent in all of us -

*Remember I am dust, and wind and shadow
and life as fleeting as the flower of grass.*
The Venerable Bede

*A great truth is a truth whose opposite is also
a great truth.*
Christopher Morley

"I have known Garry Thomson for many years now and we worked closely together when he was a vice-president of the Buddhist Society of London. I recommend this book to all students of the Buddha's teaching, especially to those who are stuck in the belief that science will one day provide us with all the answers.
This book offers us a view of the Dhamma from an intelligent and sceptical mind, giving us much to reflect on."

Venerable Ajahn Sumedho

Venerable Ajahn Sumedho

Prologue

In 1661 Robert Boyle, one of the great contributors to modern science, published his *Skeptical Chymist*. The term "sceptical" is defined in the Oxford Dictionary as "Inclined to suspense of judgement, given to questioning truth of facts and soundness of inferences". It is not to be confused, though it often is, with the term "cynical", (sneering, fault-finding).

In Thailand there is a pleasant custom, in memory of a deceased relative or friend, of putting together a book of material relevant to their lives and loves.

It occurred to me that I could save a lot of trouble if, while still alive, I myself were to put together certain scattered writings concerning the Dhamma and science and other related matters.

Being a collection of articles written over a period of 16 years, there are bound to be repetitions. These I have on occasion allowed to add emphasis.

Some readers may suggest that, while deploring the clinging to opinions, this book contains a good many opinions itself. I am not too con-

cerned about this. After all the Buddha looked on his practice as an investigation which each of us must undergo. During the course of this journey we come across varied beliefs, dogmas, opinions, some of them of
great interest. But we don't hold fast to any of them. Consequently what
concerns me more is that, over the 16-year period of these articles, my
views haven't changed enough, though they have certainly weakened!

Concerning the discussions on certain Pali words, and the free translations, I may wrongly give the impression that I am a Pali scholar. Here I
feel an imposter. I can only hope that, armed with both Childers and
Rhys Davids dictionaries, and with other important books of Theravada
study, I have been able to clarify certain aspects of the Buddha's teaching.
I have been swimming in the Dhamma for a quarter-century or so, and
have come to love it.

Maurice Walshe, in his admirable translation of the *Dīgha Nikaya*,
points out that the *Satipatthāna* (Foundations of Mindfulness, see Chapter
1) is generally regarded as the most important *sutta* in the entire Pali
Canon, that is to say the list of texts accepted by the Theravada Sangha as
the essential teaching of the Buddha. I would add, without hesitation
that it must be one of the most important documents in the world. The
reason: that it is, as far as is known, the earliest extant document to teach
the basic meditation practice, which we today find behind so many mystical teachings. Two fine translations, by Nyanaponika Mahathera[1] and by
the above-mentioned Maurice Walshe[2], are widely available. For the con-
venience of the reader new to Buddhism, I have included a brief translation in the opening chapter.

But, venerable though it is, the document cannot have been altogether immune from changes and omissions. I have attempted to clarify some
of these.

Close to the *Satipatthāna* in importance must come the talk which the
Buddha delivered to the Kalamas (ch.2). It is an amazing document,
which, however, is very seldom remembered in practice, even by

Buddhist monks, in their efforts to impart the teaching. In the résumé to be found in Chapter 2. I have drawn largely from a scholarly translation and interpretation by the Ven. Phra Khantipalo, an article to be found in the "Young Buddhist", Singapore(1982), pp.115-9[3].

I am glad of the opportunity to express my gratitude to the teaching by example given by the Ven. Sumedho, Abbot of Amaravati Buddhist Centre, and by the Theravada monks and nuns under him.

I acknowledge the kindness of the Buddhist Society, and of the Buddhist Publishing Group, who, one or the other, hold the copyright of almost all the chapters in this book, for permission to reproduce them here in revised form

1

The Satipatthāna Sutta

(This is an abbreviated version, intended to present the complete essentials of the instruction to the reader, while avoiding much of the repetition. [4])

Thus have I heard: Once the Lord was living among the Kurus at Kammāsadhamma, a market town. There he addressed the monks:

This is the one way [5], monks, for the purification of beings, for the overcoming of sorrow and lamentation, for the disappearance of pain and grief, for the attainment of the right path, for the realisation of *Nibbāna*, namely the *Satipatthāna Sutta*, the four Foundations of Awareness. What are the four?

A monk dwells watching the body (*kāya*) as the body [6], ardent, clearly comprehending and aware, having overcome hankering and craving for the world; he dwells watching the feelings(*vedanā*) as feelings, ardent, clearly comprehending and aware, having overcome hankering and brooding over the world; similarly he watches the heart/mind (*citta*) and the images of the mind (*dhamma*).

I. WATCHING THE BODY

And how, monks, does a monk watch the body as the body?

In the forest at the foot of a tree or in an empty place he sits down cross-legged, body erect, aware. Aware he breathes in and aware he breaths out. If his breathing is long he knows: long breath in, long breath out; and if his breathing is short he knows: short breath in, short breath out. He resolves: "with consciousness in the body, calming the body, I shall breathe in and breathe out [7]."

It is just like a skilled wood-turner who, whether he makes a long or short stroke, knows: "A long stroke – a short stroke."[8]

Thus he dwells watching the body as body internally or externally, or both internally and externally[9]. Or he dwells watching the beginning and the ending of the things of the body. So his awareness that "there is a body" is established just to the extent necessary for comprehension and awareness. Unattached he dwells, clinging to nothing in the world[10]. It is thus that a monk dwells watching the body as the body.

And again, a monk, when walking, knows "walking"; when standing he knows standing; when sitting he knows "sitting"; when lying down he knows "lying down". So that, however his body is disposed he is aware of how it is.

And again, a monk setting out or returning acts with full attention; looking ahead or looking around; bending and stretching; wearing the robe and carrying the almsbowl: eating, drinking, chewing and tasting;

urinating and defecating; walking, standing, sitting, falling asleep, waking, speaking or silent; in all these activities he acts with full attention[11].

And again a monk reflects on this body itself, from the soles of the feet to the crown of the head, encased in skin and full of various impurities: head hair, body hair, nails, teeth, skin, flesh, sinews, bones, marrow, kidneys, heart, liver, pleura, spleen, lungs, intestines, mesentary, stomach, faeces, bile, phlegm, pus, blood, sweat, fat, tears, serum, saliva, mucus, synovial fluid, urine.

It is as if one were to examine the contents of a double-mouthed provision bag filled with various kinds of grain: here are hill-rice, paddy, mung-beans, kidney-beans, sesame, husked rice.[12]

And again a monk reflects on the body as composed of the four elements – earth, water, fire, air – like a skilled butcher sitting at a cross-roads with a slaughtered cow divided into four portions[13].

Again, as a monk might see a body thrown aside in the charnel-ground, dead for a few days, swollen, discoloured, decomposing; later to be devoured by crows, ravens, vultures, wild dogs or jackals; after that a skeleton with some remaining flesh or sinews; the bones soon scattered; after a year or so white like sea shells; in the very end reduced to powder. So he reflects on his body, that there is no escape from the same fate[14].

Thus he dwells watching the body as the body, internally or externally, or both internally and externally. Or he dwells watching the beginning and the ending of the things of the body. Or his awareness that "there is a body" is established just to the extent necessary for comprehension and awareness. Unattached he dwells, clinging to nothing in the world.

It is thus that the monk dwells watching the body as the body.

II. WATCHING THE FEELINGS *(VEDANĀ)*
And how does a monk dwell watching the feelings?[15]

Experiencing a pleasant feeling he knows "a pleasant feeling", and similarly when experiencing a painful feeling, or a feeling which is neither pleasant or painful. Whatever the feeling he also knows whether it is related to worldly or to spiritual things.

Thus he dwells watching the feelings internally or externally, or both internally and externally. Or he dwells watching the beginning and the ending of feelings. Or his awareness that "there is feeling" is established just to the extent necessary for comprehension and awareness. Unattached he dwells, clinging to nothing in the world.

It is thus that the monk dwells watching the feelings.

III. WATCHING *CITTA*

And how does a monk watching *citta* as *citta* ?[16]

A monk recognises *citta* with attachment and *citta* without attachment; *citta* with hate and without hate; with and without delusion; shrunken *citta*; distracted *citta*, *citta* as elevated or not; as surpassable; as concentrated or unconcentrated; as free or bound.

Thus he dwells watching *citta* as *citta*; internally or externally, or both internally and externally. Or he dwells watching the beginning and the ending of states of *citta*. Or his awareness that "there is this or that state" is established just to the extent necessary for comprehension and awareness. Unattached he dwells, clinging to nothing in the world.

It is thus that the monk dwells watching *citta*.

IV. WATCHING DHAMMA

And how, monks, does a monk dwell watching Dhamma[17] ?

The following are then listed for contemplation:-

The five hindrances (sensual desire, ill-will, laziness, worry and flurry, doubt)

The five aggregates (form, *vedanā*, perception, *sankhāras*, consciousness)

The six organs of sense (eye, ear, nose, tongue, body, inner world)

The seven factors of enlightenment (*sati*, investigation, energy, rapture, tranquillity, *samādhi*, equanimity)

The Four Noble Truths

The *Sutta* ends:

Verily, monks, whoever, whether monk or nun or layperson, practises these Foundations of Awareness for seven years in this manner will either attain *Arahantship* here and now or, if there is yet a remnant of clinging, reach the state of a Non-returner.

Seven years! Seven months, seven days. Whoever practises these Foundations of Awareness for seven days in this manner will either attain *Arahantship* here and now or, if there is yet a remnant of clinging, reach the state of a Non-returner.

This is the one way, monks, for the purification of beings, for the overcoming of sorrow and lamentation, for the destruction of pain and grief, for the attainment of the right path, for the realisation of *Nibbāna*, namely the *Satipatthāna*, the four Foundations of Awareness.

Thus spoke the Blessed One. Glad in heart the monks welcomed his words.

[I should emphasize that some of the explanations given here might not be agreed by the community of Buddhist scholars.]

2
What the Buddha Taught the Kālāmas

The story goes that on his travels the Buddha came to a district called Kesaputta in the domain of the Kālāmas[18]. These Kālāmas seem to have suffered from an excess of gurus and philosophers. But word must have got around that someone really special was approaching. So a group of them went out to see the Exalted One.

After greeting the Buddha with the usual courtesies, they described to him how there seemed to be no end of preachers proclaiming their own doctrines and reviling those of their rivals. It got to the point where they doubted the lot of them.

Since the Buddha's advice to the Kālāmas was momentous in his time, and remains so today it is important to see a trustworthy English paraphrase. The Ven. Khantipalo has provided just such a paraphrase[19] to supplement the Pali Text Society's translation referred to above. I have made extensive use of this in what follows.

"Yes, Kālāmas, you may well doubt. You may well waver.

Now look you, Kālāmas, be not mislead by:"

anussāvena	Repeatedly hearing.
pāramparaya	An unbroken succession of teachers.
itikiraya	Report or hearsay.
pitakasampādanena	Conformity with scriptures.
takkahetu	Speculative theories.
mayahetu	Points of view.
ākāraparivitakkena	After reasoned reflection.
ditthinijjhanakkhantiya	Accepting a statement as true because it agrees with one's own ideas.
bhaviyarūpataya	The reputation of a guru.
samāno no garu	Accepting the word of one's teacher.

This last injunction of the Buddha's may take one's breath away, until we read on. I once referred to this *Sutta* in a talk given to a rather learned group. One of them was quick to point out that this all seemed to boil down to complete intellectual freedom to abide by ones own speculations. So this is not the end of the story. Indeed it's only a beginning. The Buddha exhorted his monks to further effort in the practice of the dhamma so that they will eventually "see for themselves"[20].

Knowing the Buddha's condemnation of the distraction and danger caused by efforts to acquire psychic powers, it is a little surprising that these were not included in the Kālāma's list. They were perhaps kept aside for a future lesson in the Dhamma [21].

I request the reader not to be deterred by a long list of Pali words, none of which will be repeated in this booklet. The list is printed in order that the interested reader can confirm the translation.

3

Essential Buddhism

All religions are true insofar as they follow the essence of those perennial teachings revealed by the Buddha, Sri Ramana Maharshi and many, many others. They become false or misleading to the extent that they depart from the universal message, as all religions inevitably seem to do in the passage of time.

The Buddha affirmed that he was but a new messenger carrying an age-old message. The first of five Buddhas is said to have arison 91 aeons (*kappa*,Skt.*kalpa*) ago[22]. One of the first things to understand when approaching his teaching is that he imposed no beliefs or doctrines of any kind on his followers, warning them indeed to test, not only what others said but even his own words (Chapter 2). How ever can one hope to test all these conflicting sermons? By the practice. The Buddha taught, not a doctrine but a practice by which earnest people may "come and see" for themselves.

It is a stunning revelation to discover, in one great teacher after another, that, whatever the words chosen, the practice reveals itself as universal in essence. From this point onwards a sturdy confidence grows in the seeker as he comes to find out that, to the mind which has become a little more lucid, words which previously seemed to mean little now shine brightly.

Because the Buddha left no creed one of the first difficulties facing a new Buddhist is how to answer the question everybody will ask: "What is Buddhism? What makes it different from other religions?" To answer in terms to be understood by everybody is to answer superficially. A Westerner might say that the Buddha taught *karma* and rebirth, novel in the West but accepted without hesitation by most of the Far East. *Karma* and rebirth are a universal background to all Indian thought, so an Indian looking to characterise Buddhism might fasten on the Buddhist "doctrine" of *Anattā* (*An-Atman* or no *Atman*). Surely the Buddha's teaching of *Anattā* could not be more opposed to the whole of the Vedanta tradition? We must explore this carefully. But first let us briefly put the Buddha's teaching into its contemporary setting.

The Buddha lived and taught in northern India, in an area roughly defined by the upper Ganges and its tributaries, about 2500 years ago. At that time orthodox religion was in the hands of the brahmins, who were responsible for administering all ceremonies and rituals, and who were also in powerful positions as advisers to heads of governments. This official religion was by then old enough to be showing signs of rigidity. When ceremony and belief become rigid they become empty. The caste system, though not yet fully developed, was certainly an essential support for the brahmins' hereditary power.

The Buddha developed a Sangha, a monastic order, open to everybody, irrespective of caste. Therein the monk could quieten his mind and open himself to the universal by simple and direct practice, unobstructed by traditional ritual. Gods were not denied, but were certainly not regarded as of direct relevance on the path to enlightenment/freedom/*nirvāna*. This was a path which each must tread by his own effort.

Anattā was an essential part of the practice and so it is important to understand what *anatta* implies. We have already noted that it is not a doctrine. When asked by the Wanderer Vachagotta: "Is there an *atman*, (or, as we might say, a soul)? The Buddha did the only thing possible to a wise man: he refused to say either yes or no. He answered in effect: "If I tell you there is no *atman* you will take me for a nihilist. If I tell you there is an *atman* you will think I'm just giving you the brahminical doctrine." He might have added that this is a mystery too deep for the human mind to fathom[23].

That great 20th century Vedanta sage, the late Sri Nisargadatta Maharaj, answers in words the Buddha might have used: "You need not know what you are. Enough to know what you are not. What you are you will never know, for every discovery reveals new dimensions to conquer."[24]

Instead of uselessly puzzling, one is to follow the practice of *anattā* as described in the *Satipatthāna sutta* (Chapter 1).

The Buddha said his teaching was like a raft. A seeker travelling through dangerous country comes to a deep river. He sees that the country on the far side is good, but he cannot get across to it. There is no ford or bridge or boat. So he sets to work to build himself a raft from the materials at hand, just to keep himself afloat. This raft is as simple as possible. There is nothing superfluous and no decoration. It is just for crossing the river. And so he paddles across, using his hands. Once on the other bank, should he keep his raft, walking forward with it on the top of his head? No! He leaves it behind and walks on unburdened. "Use my Dhamma-raft (teaching-raft) to get across the river of *saṁsāra* (continued existence). Once over, you will see and understand for yourself and so you can leave the raft behind. It will have served its purpose."[25]

But his instructions, so simple in essence are not easy to carry out. They are for the fully dedicated, and not for the lazy. I think the Buddha expected only the few, those "with little dust in their eyes" [26] to follow his teaching with all their heart. But he didn't single out intellectuals or any other group, and spoke often to ordinary people. He told them to lead honest, honourable lives, and to look up to those monks who had gone "from home to homelessness" in order that their whole lives could be bent towards clarity, awareness and compassion, and that they in their turn might spread the message to others.

Unfortunately most people demand a good deal more than admonitions. They demand explanations and beliefs, the very things the Buddha taught us not to waste time on. In a famous parable he told of the man shot by a poisoned arrow who, when his friends gathered round and sent for a doctor, shouted: "Stop! I won't have this arrow taken out until I know who shot me, and how, and all about the shooting". The Buddha left the story at that[27]. We presume the victim died. This was the warning that first things must come first: "One thing I teach – suffering and the ending of suffering."

By the time of the famous Buddhist King of India, Asoka (died 232 B.C.) ordinary Buddhists would have said, if asked, that the purpose of Buddhism for monks was to attain release from the endless round of rebirth, and for lay people to be reborn in happier circumstances. The overriding importance of the quiet mind open to the present moment became obscured by the hope of future benefits. And so it remains to this day for the most part, in most of the Buddhist world.

As well as beliefs, people need worship. The Buddha never denied the existence of deities and other supernatural beings of a more or less exalted nature[28]. Belief in God arises from our inability to understand universal love without personifying that love. The Buddha never spoke of one God: this is a mystery altogether beyond words. In the spirit of his teaching no effigy was made of the Buddha until some centuries of his death. But as we can see, things took their usual course, and now such images exist in all Buddhist countries. Indeed in Tibet before the recent Chinese invasion there was a complex pantheon of deities, though the more spiritual among the Tibetans would recognize the truth of John Blofeld's "wisdom to reconcile deep devotion to a deity with the knowledge that deities are not! [29] "

Almost every kind of religious belief is to be found somewhere under the tolerant umbrella of Buddhism. Behind so much detail the messages of the *Satipatthāna Sutta*, the raft and the poisoned arrow are often forgotten.

There are many ways of presenting the kernel of what the Buddha taught. Here is one suggestion:

"The ending of suffering through awakening, by the practice of *sati* and not clinging to anything in the world."

That simple teaching, bringing those who hear to inner stillness, has been repeated so many times, in so many places. Yet it is still heard by so few.

4

Sāti the Fisherman's Son

Thus have I heard:

Once the Lord was staying in the Jeta Grove in Anathapindika's monastery near Sāvatthi. Now there was a monk called Sāti [30], a fisherman's son, who had fallen into a mistaken belief: "The Lord says that consciousness (*viññāna*), not anything else, continues through life and from life to life."

The other monks argued with him and tried their hardest to dissuade him: "Sāti, don't misrepresent the Lord in this way. He has explained in many a figure the connection of consciousness with interdependent origination (*paticca samuppāda*). And he says that if the right conditions are not present consciousness does not arise."

But Sāti the Fisherman's Son, in spite of much pressure, kept firmly to his belief that consciousness continues through life and from life to life.

Since none of the monks were able to move him, they decided to go to the Lord and tell him the whole story. So the Lord commanded a monk to summon Sāti, who presently appeared and sat down respectfully.

"Is it true what they say of you, Sāti?"

"Yes, Lord."

"What is consciousness, Sāti?

"It is what speaks and what feels and what experiences the fruits of karma, good and bad."

"Foolish man! Who do you suppose I taught that kind of Dhamma to? Not only do you misrepresent me with your wrong attitude but you injure yourself and give rise to much woe and sorrow for yourself in the future."

Then the Lord turned to the other monks and said: "What do you think about all this? Has Sāti even a glimmering of the Dhamma and the discipline?"

"Not so! How could it be so, Lord?", they answered.

And Sāti the Fisherman's son, sat silent and ashamed, brooding, speechless, his shoulders drooping, his head bowed.

The Lord said: "Sāti, you foolish man, you will be remembered for this wrong belief."

"Monks, on account of whatever is the origin of consciousness arising, by that it is named. If consciousness arises because of an eye and material shapes, then it is known as eye-consciousness. If consciousness arises because of an ear and sounds then it is known as ear-consciousness." And similarly with the other senses, including the sixth sense (which is concerned with the interior world).

"Monks, consciousness is like fire. A fire made of wood chips is a chip fire. A fire made of grass is a grass fire, and one can have a cow-dung fire, a chaff fire or a rubbish fire. Just as a **fire** is named by what causes it to **burn**, so **consciousness** is named by what causes it to **arise**. When consciousness arises because of your eyes and the things you see, it can be called visual consciousness. When it arises because of your ears and the things you hear, it is auditory consciousness. And it is the same with the nose, the tongue, the touch and the internal sense of mental objects."

"Do you see, monks, how this comes about?"

The *Sutta* of which the above is the first part is entitled the "Greater *Sutta* on the Destruction of Craving", and is number 38 in the *Majjhima Nikāya*. The passage is a free translation intended to present the meaning of the Pali as clearly as possible. For a full and literal translation the reader should refer to the Pali Text Society's *Middle Length Sayings*.

We need to look at this story about poor Sāti with the kernel of the Buddha's teaching always in mind: give up clinging, and in particular don't cling to any beliefs. Why? Because you will find that all suffering has its roots in clinging.

The Theravada *suttas* reached their final form over a period which may have extended to a few centuries, during which time the Buddha's teaching must inevitably have become a little dimmed and adulterated. According to scholarly opinion early and late elements may be mixed, even in a single *sutta*. We can never, of course be sure in our attempts to separate early from late. But we may suspect lateness if we find that things have rigidified into cathechistic lists and set philosophical forms. The Buddha taught, not philosophical opinion but spiritual experience, and in a simple straightforward language using everyday words. We can suspect lateness even more strongly where we find doctrinal tendencies. This *sutta* stands on a fascinating borderline.

His fellow monks upbraid Sāti for holding a wrong belief, a wrong doctrine. Forget for the moment what that wrong doctrine was. That they told him it was wrong implies that they thought they knew of a right doctrine which his contradicted.

There seems nothing strange in this to a Westerner. After all, religions are their belief systems, are they not? Therefore Buddhists, like the members of any other religion, must have a creed, a list of beliefs which they regard as undeniably true? Indeed the Eightfold Path is headed by *Sammā Ditthi*, which is usually translated as Right or Perfect View. Perhaps, on consideration, the choice of the word View rather than Belief may imply that there was a certain uneasiness in the minds of the English translators. They knew very well how forthright had been the Buddha's warning against clinging to any belief. Now they had to square that with a teaching, *Sammā Ditthi*, which the Buddha traditionally propounded in his very first sermon: that *Sammā Ditthi* consists of the Four Noble Truths. Now holding a certain point of view implies rather less than being ready to die for one's creed so, says the translator, let us translate *Ditthi* as Views. But is not this in itself "a wriggling and scuffling of beliefs", to use the Buddha's words? Surely we would be wise to take on trust at least the Four Noble Truths and the Three Signs of Being (*Anicca, Anattā* and *Dukkha*) until such time as we arrive at the truth ourselves. But would the Buddha have approved even this minimal doctrinal base?

One need only go back to what scholars regard as one of the earliest of the scriptures to find the Buddha adamant that one should adhere to no beliefs of any kind: the stanza quoted at the head of Chapter 12 on belief is characteristic:

"Nothing is assumed nothing is rejected. He has washed all beliefs away." (*Sutta Nipāta*, stanza 787)

This refrain is repeated again and again in different forms. But the earliest monks, just like ourselves, found it a hard struggle. We have to say that they seem to have lost that struggle. Signs of retreat from the teachings of the *Sutta Nipāta* may perhaps be seen in *suttas* like this one about poor Sāti.

What may have happened is that Sāti insisted on retaining the ordinary belief of the day, arguing in this kind of way: "My consciousness is me; I may in the very long run be impermanent, but I'm obviously permanent from moment to moment, from day to day. And why not from life to life? Otherwise we wouldn't be able to talk about the rebirth of a particular person." He uses the word 'consciousness' (*viññāna*) to identify this apparently permanent entity. We cannot, however, precisely define *viññāna* as used in the Theravada scriptures, at any rate the earlier ones. Usually it has that loose meaning that it has today in non-philosophical speech: 'consciousness' is what speaks and experiences.

His fellow monks must have become worried at the tenacity with which he held onto his belief. They tried – we hope – to express in various ways how there will always be mysteries beyond the reach of the mind. The text says they threw the *Paticca Samuppāda* (Law of Interdependent Origination) at him, though this list is not to be found in its twelvefold form in the earliest *suttas*.

But Sāti stood his ground, and so the Buddha was petitioned to explain consciousness. He used for this purpose a powerful analogy which recalls his famous Fire Sermon ("Monks, all is burning!")[31].

The key sentence is: "Just as a **fire** is named by what causes it to **burn**, so **consciousness** is named by what causes it to **arise**." The Pali reader may confirm (*Majjhima Nikāya* I, p.259) that, though considerable liberties have been taken in rearrangement, this is the literal sense of the instruction.

The sense data are the fuel which give rise to the fire of consciousness. **No fuel, no fire. No sense data, no consciousness.** Remember that sense data include all the images in the ever-active mind as well as those from the outside world. In the normal course of life, consciousness arises quite as frequently in the mind as in the eye, the ear or the sense of touch. But this all happens so quickly that it is hard to follow.

As I write this in a room filled with quiet conversation, the traffic flowing below the window, consciousness travels from thoughts about Sāti to snatches of conversation overheard, to glimpses of taxis and buses, to irrelevant mental associations. Sometimes it lingers as intended on the matter in hand (the writing of this article), but the next moment it is flitting as quickly as a hover-fly from one sense-gate to the next. But what have I just said? Through long habit I have been talking about consciousness travelling and lingering and flitting, just as if it were continuous. This falsehood was what the Buddha put his finger on. Consciousness, like fire, is discontinuous. It arises when there is fuel.

We find this hard to believe. We prefer to think that consciousness moves like a searchlight examining what is seen, what is heard, what is thought. Now we are asked to find out through meditation whether it is not the other way round. Perhaps what is sensed switches on the searchlight.

It may occur to the reader that Sāti should have said: "Yes Lord! I understand my mistake. *Viññāna* is indeed discontinuous. I should have said *atta*, self, not *viññāna*. But this would only have earned for him a further rebuke from the Buddha, a reminder of what he said in answer to Vachagotta's query[32]: that claiming that a self exists or that there is no self, both are equally wrong-headed. The mystery is too deep for the mind to fathom.

What about dreamless sleep? We prefer to hold all kinds of opinion about what we might then be doing. But perhaps "I" am not anywhere in dreamless sleep.

When we faint we are willing to admit: "I lost consciousness"; but only because we assume this is shorthand for "I lost consciousness of my surroundings."

Alright I can see the body is not me because I can observe it. But surely it's mine! Feelings of bodily pleasure and pain, if not too strong, can be observed as "not me", especially in meditation. And it is possible to watch the workings of the mind, pre-eminently the constantly recurring "I want". But, grasping creatures that we are, it's much more difficult to give up the feeling of ownership.

One simply cannot comprehend the cessation of consciousness except as total death, and even that is a difficult imaginative feat. But this is the time for doing the Dhamma, not talking about it. After all, the Buddha told us, although it seems to be in flat contradiction, that to talk of the annihilation of self is yet another way of falling back into beliefs. Look and see with the quiet mind whether or not consciousness dies and reappears from moment to moment. Look and see what really goes on, with patience and often with amusement.

Clearly all this makes no philosophical sense. The message which the Buddha had to put across is indeed "difficult to comprehend, against the stream"[33]. We all find ourselves ranged behind Sāti in his perplexity. Far better, indeed, to acknowledge this frankly than to imagine that we understand.

It is necessary to keep reminding ourselves that this is not just some kind of intellectual game. We are concerned with cutting through the veil of illusion here and now: the most important task in the world. So let us finally try our woefully inadequate minds on the following:

> "Friend, just as two bundles of reeds were to stand supporting the other, even so consciousness is dependent on name-and-form, and name-and-form is dependant on consciousness. . .But, friend, if one of these two bundles of reeds were to be removed the other would fall down. . .Even so,

friend, with the cessation of consciousness name-and-form
ceases; with the cessation of name-and-form consciousness
ceases...Thus comes about the cessation of this entire mass of
suffering[34]".

Name-and-form (*Nāmarūpa*) is a word used by both Buddhist and
Vedanta sages. It is defined, not by statements in a dictionary but by spiritual experience. With the help of Bhikkhu Nanananda[35] (see page 55) it
will suffice for our present purpose to say that "form" refers to the apparent forms of the external world, including our body, while "name" covers
our reaction, both in naming and feeling the objects we encounter.

Now the Buddha takes us one step further. The world which I divide
into named objects and "me" is so intertwined that with one absent the
other ceases to be. When one bundle of reeds is removed the other falls
down. *Nāmarūpa* is one word, and this serves to remind us that the external world and the internal world are the same. What would Sāti have
made of this?

One mistake has often been made. We must avoid it at all costs. It is to
take the complete record of what the Buddha is reported to have said,
and to try to weld it into one coherent philosophy, one intellectually con-
sistent structure in which nothing clashes with anything else. When the
matter in hand is spiritual guidance, statements are always being made
which clash logically. As is well known, Zen monks make use of clashing
logic to confuse the mind and so lead beyond.

The Buddha leads us beyond by giving us a simple practice. We can
still the mind and we can watch.

5

Buddhism and Science

During the 20th century an unhealthy situation has developed. While the discoveries of science are put to ever more dangerous use, only a tiny proportion of the world's population understands what scientists are up to. Most of the world's rulers share this ignorance. As has frequently been remarked, scientists appear as the priesthood of a new cult. Despite the skilful efforts of scientific journalists, the public appetite inclines towards quack science – plants with psychic powers, spoon bending, visitors from outer space, and so on.

As followers of a religion which, far from having to retreat before the advance of science, welcomes all kinds of exploration, we have a particular duty to appraise the achievements of science with coolness and equanimity, to admonish the over-credulous as well as to establish the limitations of materialism.

Among writers about Buddhism and science there are those who seem to suggest that the greatness of the Buddha lay in his having knowledge of a kind only now being revealed by scientists. And indeed the psychological insights of the Buddhist scriptures appear very modern in their analysis of perception and feeling (see also Chapter 8). But to admire the Buddha because he foresaw some discoveries of science is to over-exalt a minor aspect of the Dhamma. There are others who maintain that scientists are at last coming round to "what we knew all along": a belief in all kinds of supernatural phenomena. But the Buddha, neither denying nor affirming, discouraged investigation of psychic powers[21].

I suggest that we can find a deeper and more fruitful relation between Buddhism and science.

First we need to take a brief look at the scientific method and the realm of scientific knowledge.

The scientist attempts to advance knowledge by constructing a hypothesis: a proposed explanation of facts which have been ascertained by experiment. This hypothesis builds on the established body of scientific knowledge, all of which can be checked by any group of suitably-qualified scientists at any time. His hypothesis is only useful if it can suggest further experiments designed, not to verify it, but to probe it for faults. A hypothesis can never be demonstrated true. It just becomes stronger and stronger the more tests it passes. Thus the hypothesis proposed by Newton, which is the foundation of astronomy, that the gravitational force of attraction between two bodies is proportional to the product of their masses and inversely proportional to the square of the distance between their centres, has passed so many tests that it is now known as the Law of Gravity.

A hypothesis that is so vague and imprecise as to be untestable is of no value. Examples of scientifically useless hypotheses abound from the early days of science. Democritus (c.470-380 B.C.) held correctly that the world consists of atoms ever moving in empty space. Asanga, a Mahayana Buddhist philosopher of the 4th century A.D. proposed a similar atomic theory. However these insights remained barren since they yielded no measurable predictions which could be tested. A scientifically useful atomic theory had to await the work of Dalton at the beginning of the nineteenth century.

A very good example of hypothesis and testing, and a particularly good one from our point of view because it may lead us beyond the borders of established science, is Rupert Sheldrake's hypothesis of "formative causation" [35].

There is an awkward gap in present-day scientific knowledge, which is not acknowledged as frankly as it should be in popular accounts. Most readers will be familiar with the existence of genes, the instruments of heredity. In the nucleus of every single cell in every single person is an almost identical set of genes: about 100,000 working genes in humans. The genes are said not only to build the body in the first place, but to keep it in good repair. Each gene manufactures one particular protein. The proteins form not only the muscles but also all the chemical switches which start and stop our various internal manufacturing processes. There once seemed to be so many genes that even the daunting complexity of an animal's body plus its built-in instinctive behaviour could be explained by this simple mechanism alone. Then it was discovered that there were long lengths of gene with no apparent function and that there were multiple copies of genes with a lot of work to do. Consequently the information stored in the genes is many times smaller than was first supposed. Nevertheless orthodox theory asks us to believe that both the form and the function of all beings arises through cells of different types multiplying in accordance with the switching on or off of the various genes. The popularity among almost all scientists of such reductionist theories as this can be ascribed to the extraordinary success of the principle of parsimony, Occam's razor. William of Occam (died 1347) advised that all unnecessary constituents should be cut away from explanations as with a razor. In other words we are to choose the simplest hypothesis to fit the facts, based on what is known and acknowledged.

Occasionally this may put us in the situation of a mythical TV operator who, though totally ignorant of the existence of radio waves, is confident that he can understand where the voices and pictures in the TV come from. He takes the TV set carefully apart and is able to demonstrate that a voltage applied at certain points produces an audible blip in the speaker or flash of light on the screen. And, of course, he names all the parts large and small. His argument then runs: "The voices and pictures are produced by the applied voltage acting through various electronic devices. We don't understand it fully at the moment, but we've worked it out in principle. There's no need to invoke your supernatural radio waves."

Sheldrake offers us a theory relating to how all complex patterns are formed, whether organic molecules, the bodies of plants and animals, or even patterns of behaviour. He simply proposes that, once a pattern has been formed, in whatever way, by that very act it becomes more likely that this same pattern will appear again. By the time millions of the same pattern have been formed (of an ant, for instance), or of the mating behaviour of some animal, this particular pattern will have become firmly fixed. Note that Sheldrake offers no explanation, supernatural or otherwise, of how this all might work. He simply proposes it as a hypothesis for the scientific community to test by experiment.

Those with a stake in the beyond, as one might say, warm to the theory. It seems to take a knock at materialist science and to verify our intuitive feeling that the manifest world is a projection of something greater, higher and more mysterious. But we must remember that, as Sheldrake himself has emphasized, his proposals are far-reaching but tentative and must await experimental findings.

The scientific method, then, involves gathering experimental facts, and then forming a hypothesis. This must (a) fit the facts, (b) be testable by other scientists, and (c) usefully extend our knowledge of the natural world.

There is another characteristic that grows out of this: a hypothesis is a mental model. Science is the making of mental models. Werner Heisenberg, one of the great 20th-century physicists, has expressed this in a different way: that the laws of nature no longer deal with elementary particles but with the knowledge of these particles, that is with the contents of our minds! But I doubt if many of us realize, scientists or not, the extent to which we all deal with the world by making mental models of it. As soon as we start talking about the earth revolving around the sun, our contact with the real earth beneath our feet and the real sun above our heads is diminished, to be replaced by a little mental model or picture of spinning balls. We think about future events very often by setting up a little theatre in our heads with "me" the principle actor, and we imagine the dialogues that will take place. Of course we don't actually picture the stage of a theatre, but this is what it amounts to.

A third characteristic of science is the central place that mathematics holds in it. And this is where most of us get left behind. Hypotheses are often enunciated in mathematical form: another kind of (more abstract) mental model-making, though perhaps mathematics is better described as a language. You describe your model in mathematical language and follow the rules and methods of mathematics to establish that such-and-such a cause will be followed by such-and-such an effect. These predictions are then translated back into ordinary language so that they can be tested.

The development of the laser has followed this pattern. But perhaps the best example of the power of purely mathematical hypothesis-making is the black hole. We've all heard so much about black holes that we could be excused in supposing that some have been discovered. Indeed black holes have become increasingly accepted by cosmologists as real physical objects. But so far none have convincingly been shown to exist. They remain the creation of pure mathematical theory.

What if we do our mathematics and then find we can't translate the result back into this world of things we think we can comprehend? This happens more often than scientists like to admit. Consider even the elementary treatment of energy. A moving object has energy by virtue of its motion. This is something we can grasp: a travelling bullet would appear to have a great deal of energy. But there is also potential energy, energy of position. A child throws a ball up in the air so that it just lodges in the gutter. Lying at rest in the gutter, the figures will only work out right if we say that all the energy of motion (kinetic energy) given to the ball by the child has now been converted into another kind of energy: potential energy. But the ball is at rest. Where is its energy now? This is all meaningless outside mathematics, but most scientists have used the formulae so often that they have forgotten to be puzzled.

It is equally puzzling that light must sometimes be regarded as waves and sometimes as particles. Light is at the same time both particles and waves: pure particles, pure waves, not some hybrid mixture. Light appears as particles or waves according to the experimental arrangement. This we cannot imagine.

"Physics is mathematical", said Bertrand Russell," not because we know so much about the physical world, but because we know so little: it is only its mathematical properties that we can discover" [36].

"In mathematics you don't understand things. You just get used to them".

(John von Neumann, frequently described as the father of the modern computer)

One last word about the direction that science is travelling along. Having striven to confine themselves to the natural world, the further scientists look in the direction of the very large (cosmology) or of the very small (particle physics) the more mysterious and unimaginable space, time and matter become. In an attempt to translate mathematical statements into ordinary language, the universe is described in a well-known phrase: "a four-dimensional space/time continuum". Gravitation is said to curve this space/time. But of course, outside mathematics time is fundamentally different from space, and you can only curve things in space, not space itself. Even more surprising, it has been speculated that the ultimate constituents of matter may be dimensionless points: not just very small particles but particles with no size at all! Having become accustomed to being told that solid matter is mostly space, we may now have to accept that it is all space (see also Chapter 13).

Though they may sometimes give the opposite impression, scientists are as puzzled as lay people by these mysteries.

Having got this far we begin to see that there are big differences between Buddhism and science, both in what they regard as primary knowledge and in their methods of coming to that knowledge. To the scientist, primary knowledge is that hard-won corpus of facts and explanations which has been built up by reason and experiment. The Buddhist allows this knowledge but holds it of small account compared with the wisdom and compassion that comes about through the practice of the Dhamma. The scientist asks for a description of this wisdom and, when told that it is inexpressible but relates to the oneness of life, answers that this doesn't amount to real knowledge at all. The scientist plans his acquisition of knowledge with his intellect working at full power. The Buddhist sets up the conditions and lets wisdom happen in stillness.

But the most revolutionary difference – and here it is the Buddha who seems to present-day people to be the revolutionary – is in the matter of mental model-making. The scientist is the big chief of mental model-makers. Furthermore he is entitled to say, "My models work. They really do correspond to the real world." Indeed they do: a highly theoretical model of protons and neutrons turned Hiroshima to dust. Yet the very essence of the Buddhist approach – *sati*, awareness – is seeing the present moment as it is, without interposing any interpretation, any mental model. As far as possible all memories and judgements, the reasoning and feeling mind itself, are all left to rest. How can one ever learn anything from such a practice? The scientist can be excused his impatience.

In spite of all this, the curious fact is that science and Buddhism get along extraordinarily well together and seem to compliment each other. So let us look at some of these pregnant areas of agreement.

(1) Space and time. Many of the older among us learnt plenty about hell as children. But in spite of lavish use of the word "everlasting" the Western world has only recently got to grips with large numbers, thanks to science. To man who is said to be the "measure of all things" ideas of immense areas of space and time, dwarfing our own lifespan, come uneasily. Only three and a half centuries ago Bishop Ussher announced the date of creation as 4004 B.C., and even today there are those who belief that the earth was literally created in seven days. By contrast India has always been in tune with *kalpas* of time. In a standard calculation 1 *kalpa*, a day and a night of Brahma = 4,320,000,000 years, amazingly commensurate, if true, with present estimates of the age of our Solar System (about 4.5 billion years). As if to emphasize the point, the Chinese observer has traditionally been portrayed by artists as a tiny figure in the landscape.

(2) Computers, so their advocates say, will take over the drudgery but leave the interesting, creative, work to humans. But is this the way things are going? The pride of the Western world is in intellectual attainment. Surely difficult intellectual work will always need humans. Indeed? Computers now challenge top chess players and rival the power

of the specialist doctor in diagnosis. So it seems that computers have had their greatest successes at the top of the intellectual ladder, the end which, it has been supposed, sets us farthest above the animals. At the other end of the scale, the animal end, progress in robotics has been slow and disappointing. Robots can't even see properly. And as for imitating the ability of the humblest insect as it dashes about in search of food: that is completely beyond present-day technology (but perhaps not for long). Something momentous and very upsetting to the pride of *Homo sapiens* is becoming blurred. Is the intellect really a very much "higher" faculty than, for example, affection?

All this causes not the least distress to Buddhists, who have never drawn a division between humans and other sentient beings. As for our proud intellect, the body/mind is all *suddha sankhara puñjo*, just a lot of processes. Remember the nun Vajira's riposte to Mara, the Tempter [37]:

> Why do you harp on the word "person"?
> You are falling back on beliefs.
> There is nothing but a lot of processes.
> Put together a lot of parts and you get what is called a "chariot".
> Put together the *khandhas* and you get what is called a "person".

(3) It may be that Einstein was the last great scientist who hated defeat by paradox. We have mentioned that light must sometimes be treated as waves, sometimes as particles. Since Einstein's time such paradoxes have multiplied. Scientists have come to accept the situation described in the story of the blind men, each of whom grasped a different part of the elephant and so came away with descriptions of the animal, each true from one point of examination, but all incompatible with each other. The whole truth can never be encompassed at one and the same time. Paradox, as every practitioner of Zen knows, is a powerful tool for transcending the intellect.

(4) Science is an exploration. The Dhamma is an exploration, This brings us to the crux of the matter: rejection of fixed beliefs.

Scepticism is too often confused with cynicism. The cynic is a sneering fault-finder. The original Sceptics were the followers of Pyrro, a Greek who lived in the time of Alexander the Great. Pyrro maintained that certain knowledge on any matter was unattainable and that suspension of judgement was true wisdom. A Sceptic, according to Pyrro, is one who thinks for himself and is not satisfied simply with another's testimony. Pyrro is recorded as having studied in India. Then it is perhaps not so surprising that his attitude is so strikingly Buddhist. One is tempted to speculate that wind of the Buddha's sermon to the Kālāmas (see Chapter 3) may have blown all the way to Greece. "Monks, do you not speak that which is known by yourselves, seen by yourselves, found by yourselves?" [38]

Naturally scientists too would describe themselves as sceptics. But the sad fact is that both Buddhists and scientists fall short of the sceptical ideal. Scientists are on the whole conventional and subscribe to a widely and strongly held framework of beliefs and attitudes. Such a cluster of background beliefs is sometimes referred to as a paradigm. The current scientific paradigm embraces materialism. A materialist can be as dogmatic as any religious fanatic.

Buddhists of whatever school all tend to take on board a load of unnecessary beliefs. I'm not thinking only of a too ready credulity concerning certain doubtful health cures, or of abductions by flying saucer aliens, but also of the ossification of the Buddha's teaching aids into dogmas.

Suppose you're expounding the Four Noble Truths and somebody says "I don't believe thirst (*tanhā*) is the origin of suffering. Surely the suffering after a car crash comes directly from pain." Examine your reaction. Is it a hasty hunt for counter arguments? Must the Second Noble Truth be defended like a citadel? Surely this is slipping back into dependence on beliefs, *ditthi*. Or do you now develop the Second Noble Truth as a teaching aid in understanding pain: that the root of pain is the trying to get away from it, the thirst for freedom from pain. Similarly *anattā* is to be regarded, not as a doctrine that the self does not exist, but as a practice: the practice of examining every aspect of the body/mind to see if it is me" or "mine".

Finally we need to look again at the relation between science and Buddhism, because together they give us a set of tools for exploring the world, inner and outer.

Both are dedicated to an unbiassed, undoctrinal examination of phenomena, while both are constantly slipping back towards that all-too-human tendency to load the mind with fixed beliefs.

Both regard knowledge as of no value unless it can be verified, though they have very different approaches to verification. For the scientist this means repeating an experiment. For the Buddhist it is the still mind "seeing for oneself".

Positively no scientific discovery can shake the Buddhist, whether this relates to the outside world or the mind. This is not because the Buddhist has built an opaque wall of faith round the self but because we thrive on exploration and discovery.

6

Involvement

Those who think that it is easy to decide the extent to which Buddhists should be involved in social action have perhaps forgotten Mencken's Law. Mencken's Law states that for every complex problem there is a simple solution. . . and it is wrong! With that in mind we need to do all we can to aim at a balanced view.

The debate is usually put in the form of a question: should Buddhists be involved in social action? Have we not, right at the start, uncovered a hidden assumption: That all Buddhists should do the same thing?

Put like this, few people would agree with it.

Our unhidden assumption should be that Buddhists naturally range along a whole spectrum of attitudes, on social action as on other matters.

We must certainly throw into the dustbin the idea that all Buddhists must do the same thing. Ken Jones, in the November 1985 issue of The Buddhist Society of London's *Middle Way*, disclosed a social action spectrum. Let's try to visualise this spectrum, first of all marking out the extremes.

At one end might be the person who tries to use Buddhism solely for personal attainment and even occult power, with no concern for anybody else – a type unfortunately not unknown among so-called Buddhists. At the other end are to be found people so convinced that Buddhism is the only right way that they naturally conclude everyone must become Buddhists. And the end can be used to justify the means. Conceivably mild forms of coercion might be discussed.

Nearer the centre on the non-action side is a quite commonly encountered kind of Buddhist who, through shyness or lack of confidence, remains a secret Buddhist and can't come out and share the Dhamma with anybody else.

On the other side of centre is the peaceful activist, who has yet no understanding of the contemplative life.

But most of us are in a central, Middle-Way kind of position, with a niggling feeling of guilt at not contributing more.

My own formula for the individual might run something like this: Buddhist practice is centred on the Eight-fold Path, and the Eight-fold Path is centred on the practice of *sati*, awareness. From this centre you follow your abilities, emphasizing either action or contemplation. But this situation can't altogether be planned, shouldn't be planned. If someone asks you for help you give it to them as best you can. If opportunities for contemplation arise then they are taken.

And we'd do well to remember Dogen:

> To study the dhamma is to study the self;
> To study the self is to forget the self.

This is no mere neat epigram. Study of the self in the *sati* practice (the self, not myself) leads to understanding of how everybody's mind works. And from there grows true compassion. On the matter of compassion, *sati* does seem to be the clearest course of action. Just about the most useless thing you can say is "Love thy neighbour as thyself", without any instruction on how compassion arises. The whole violent history of Western civilisation shows this command to be actually counter-productive. And the command is echoed by certain enthusiasts who say: "Thou shalt be involved in social action." Social action enthusiasts tend, obviously, to be active people – often very active in spreading their views; occasionally perhaps even a little coercive. Contemplatives tend in the other direction; tend not to interfere with others even when they could help. Polarisation increases when the activist gets to work on the contemplative and the contemplative gets upset. Introverted contemplatives can deliver very destructive and aggressive and unholy criticism if aroused.

Up to this point we've been looking at the spectrum of social action for an individual. We have to get it quite clear that the rules are not the same for groups, such as the various Buddhist sects and societies. For example, whereas the individual appears to be free, the group is much less so:

A Buddhist group must surely cater for a wide variety of people. Such a group is inevitably involved in social action, but should not be involved in politics.

Let me expand. The very teaching of the Dhamma is a powerful source of social action, ultimately the most powerful form the world may ever know. So any group that teaches Buddhism is right in the middle of action. But that's not the end of the story: there are still important questions of how far the spreading of the Dhamma involves propaganda (now called publicity) and of how much the group should be formally linked with regular social action organisations. But involved we are.

The second point concerns politics. There is a form of argument which seeks to undermine your opposition to a certain action by pointing out that you're already involved in that action. For example, I have just undermined any Buddhist Society opposition to social action by pointing out that the Buddhist Society is already involved in social action because its declared purpose is to spread Buddhism. The same argument has been used about politics. It's evident that politics can be so loosely defined that we could be said to be involved in politics at every Council Meeting of the Buddhist Society. You can say that politics is decision-making and the coordination of power. But when it is this loosely defined it ceases to be a useful word. Let's for goodness' sake keep to the Oxford Dictionary definition of "Politics": "The science and art of government", where "government", again following Oxford, means "governing a State". Each of us is involved with politics when we vote. But the Buddhist Society does not have a vote, and should not be involved in politics. At the very least this would inject elements of dogma and coercion completely foreign to the Dhamma. But we're still not quite out of the woods.

On cross-party but still political opinions, again the Society should take no stand: nuclear disarmament, for example. Probably a large majority of members want to ban the bomb and disarm unilaterally. That's fine: let them peacefully demonstrate without either hindrance or encouragement. Again I can't imagine any Buddhists not being in favour of animal welfare. But the Society itself must stand aside from the issue: there are always other points of view which should not be disallowed. Members will obviously discuss political matters among themselves, but the Middle Way is meant for other purposes.

Two points to end on:

Firstly we must constantly bear in mind the illusory nature of individuality and free-will. Our actions, seemingly dictated by our conscious selves, are the end results of causes, within and without ourselves, of which we are not aware. Recall the waves of the sea: a wave appears to be a separate being moving forward. Yet we know that this is not so: the water moves up and down in the same place and the separate moving wave is an illusion. Consciousness, the "I" feeling, is only a tiny part of the activity of the mind. Most of this activity is unconscious. So "I" am more realistically compared just to the evanescent froth on the very surface of the wave! This realisation doesn't lead us to abdicate all responsibility for our actions. In practice it clarifies decision because of the reduced importance of "me". But it should remind us of our relative powerlessness and of the mystery of our being.

Secondly, mystics of all religions proclaim that the contemplative life is the fountainhead. Few readers, I imagine, would disagree. By the same token, whether we recall Jung's collective unconscious or remind ourselves of the ocean and its waves, an individual's acts are not separated from the community. For all its apparent inaction, the contemplative life can be called the central form of social action.

We recognise and are grateful for this fountainhead – the contemplative life – and, without making a big fuss about it, we do what we are each fitted to do.

Let our thoughts rest on the inspiring figure of His Holiness the Dalai Lama, necessarily involved in political confrontation with one of the world's cruellest states.

7

Busier than Ever!

"And what do you do with yourself now that you're retired?"

It seems that the correct answer to this question is: "Oh! I'm busier than ever!"

But I'm not busier than ever. I've now been retired for almost ten years and I'm glad of the extra time for quietness this has given me, though I should be making better use of it.

Let's try to look, as Buddhists, at this question of "spending" time. Should we so structure our day that there is little chance for boredom or guilt to arise? Is being busier than ever just a few steps up from "Oh! I've no time to meditate."?

The Buddha said that the Dhamma was for the energetic, not for the lazy, and energy is one of the five *indriya* or moral qualities. But he also said that to be fond of activity is one of the six things that make the practice of *sati* impossible[39]. At first sight these look like contradictory statements.

However, although the energetic person is usually thought of as in constant movement, there is a difference between energy and activity. We've got to be active at least part of the time, in a way that concentrates all our mental resources, whether organizing a party or writing a computer program. Perhaps a better word for energy is drive, a readiness to do what is required. Energy can be applied to bringing the mind to *sati*, stillness. Activity obviously cannot. And, since *sati* is a full-time practice, energy is obviously a necessity.

Whether or not we do a lot of work or see a lot of friends or lead a solitary life depends very much on our circumstances and on what type of person we are. But on the necessity for *sati* there can be no compromise.

Sati can mean being fully aware of the external world and of the body's movements in it.

Sati can be watching the first quick responses of pleasure or displeasure to objects coming into consciousness.

Sati can show up the mood, whether happy or downcast, angry or sad, active or lazy, bold or fearful.

Sati means quietly watching without judgement the inner world of the mind as attentively as the outer world; being aware of thoughts as they arise without being carried along by them; discovering the foolish reasoning, excuses, ego-inflation, imaginary arguments, readiness to blame others, that are always going on; seeing that the world of *dukkha* is the world of the ego.

None of this is easy. I've been practising *sati* for years and my mind's still full of an awful lot of rubbish. Yet the Buddha gave us this gift as the royal road to awakening.

8

The Honey-Cake.

Excerpts from *Sutta* 18 of the *Majjhima-Nikaya* ("Middle Length Sayings"):

"What is this teaching, Bhante, whereby, in this world of *devas*, of Mara and Brahma, of recluses and brahmans, you do not dispute with anyone? How is it, moreover, that, unyoked from desire, free from doubt, remorse destroyed, devoid of craving for any form of *bhava* (the ever changing flow of life), you are not tempted by (our perception of the world)?"

"If, O bhikkhu, one neither delights in, nor asserts, nor clings to, that which makes one subject to *papañca-saññā-sankha*, [see below] then that in itself is the end of any susceptibility to attachment, repugnance, *ditthi* (beliefs), perplexity, pride, *avijjā* (spiritual ignorance) and attachment to *bhava*. That in itself is the end of taking the stick, taking a weapon, quarrelling, contending, disputing, accusation, slander and lying speech. Here it is that all these evil *akusala* (unhealthy, unhelpful) states cease without residue."

Thus spoke the Lord, the Wellfarer. And he rose from his seat and entered the monastery. The monks said to each other: "The Lord has given us this short talk without fully explaining its meaning, and then left us. Who can explain the meaning in full?"

Then it occurred to them to go to the venerable Kaccano the Great and ask him for a full explanation.

The venerable Kaccano the Great spoke thus:

"I understand the full meaning to be as follows:

Visual *viññāna* (consciousness) arises because of the eye and material shapes. The meeting of the three is *phasso* (contact). *Vedanā* (feeling) arises because of *phasso*. What one feels one perceives. What one perceives one thinks about (*vitakka*). What one thinks about one turns into *papañca*. Due to *papañca* one is assailed by *papañca-saññā-sankha* in regard to material shapes seen by the eye, belonging to the past, the present and the future. And, brethren, the same sequence applies to hearing, smelling, touching, tasting and *mano* (the 6th sense: the sensing of the contents of the mind)."

[Later the monks asked the Buddha whether Kaccano the Great had explained correctly. He replied:]

"Monks, Kaccano the Great is of much wisdom. If you had questioned me as to the teaching I would have explained it precisely as he did. This indeed is the exact meaning and thus should you understand it."

This said, the Venerable Anando addressed the Exalted One:

"Lord, as a man overcome by hunger and exhaustion might come upon a honey-cake, tasting from each bit a delicious sweet flavour – even so, Lord, would an able-minded monk, examining with *pañña* (wisdom), get delight and satisfaction from each bit of this Dhamma-discourse. What shall it be called, Lord?"

"As you suggest, Anando, you may call this the Honey-cake discourse."

What follows is not an orthodox commentary on the *Sutta* but an attempt to study this timeless document from our standpoint in the twentieth century.

We must first try to understand the nature of the question asked of the Buddha. Rephrased it runs:

Even though you are perfectly free of the faults listed, does not the very act of perceiving the world form attachments to it?

The Buddha answers by putting his finger on the trouble: *papañca-saññā-sankha*. To dispose of the word *sankha* first, and following Ñananan-da [40], it can be taken to mean 'characterised by': *saññā* characterised by *papañca*: perception with a restless mind.

Papañca is a pivotal word in the Dhamma. It means the way the mind, never still, jumps around like a monkey from tree to tree trying and rejecting one fruit after another. *Papañca* can be contrasted to *sati*, the practice of the still mind. "If", says the Buddha, "one finds no delight in *papañca*, that in itself is the end of attachment and all that binds us to *dukkha*". He then left his disciples in a somewhat dazed condition, wondering why he had talked about not clinging to *papañca* without telling them how.

They decided to ask Kaccano the Great, who filled out the Buddha's words. What he said looks to us at first glance like psychological theory. It is not. We would do well to remember at this stage that the Buddha never expounded any teaching that was to be regarded as doctrine or theory. Everything he taught was as an aid to practice. The "Honey-cake" is no exception.

The stages enumerated by the Buddha and Kaccano as leading to *papañca-saññā-sankha* happen every moment of the waking day and are as follows:

One of the sense-organs (e.g.the eye) senses the world.

Viññāna (consciousness, e.g. eye consciousness) arises.

Meeting of the three (the world, the eye, *viññāna*) = *phasso*.

Feeling – *vedanā*.

Perception – *sañjanati*(the verb form of *saññā*), he perceives.

Thinking – *vitakka*.

Papañca... and so on.

These stages apply to each of the senses, including the sixth sense, that which sees the objects in the mind. The order is important even though the whole process takes only a fraction of a second.

Taking the example of the eye as the pre-eminent sense, all that are required in the first stage are open eyes and something to look at. Nothing unexpected here. But, in the second stage, what is this *viññāna* (consciousness) which only manifests itself through one of the senses?[41] In another *sutta* of the *Majjhima-Nikāya* (No.38. See Chapter 4) the Buddha explains to Sati the fisherman's son that *viññāna* is like a fire which requires fuel, the fuel for *viññāna* being the sense organ and its messages. A dead eye records an image on its retina and a camera records its image on a film. This is stage one: there is no *viññāna* in the dead eye or in the camera. But in the living eye *viññāna* starts from here.

The next stage is *phasso*, usually translated as 'contact'. The image on the retina of the eye immediately undergoes processing, starting at the retina itself and continuing in the visual cortex of the brain. Edges, move-ment, distances and colours are mapped out. All this occurs far below the level of consciousness. We need not suppose that the Buddha knew the details revealed by today's physiology, but his acute introspection must have shown him that the version of the world which comes out of this process into our fully conscious perception is very different to what goes in. Something very crucial is going on and I think we may assume that this is what he termed *phasso*.

Phasso leads to *vedanā*, and here is something strange. *Vedanā*, feeling, comes before *saññā* usually translated as perception. How can we have a pleasant or unpleasant feeling for something before we perceive it?

It is usually supposed that when our eyes light upon something we first recognize what it is, and then we respond with feeling to it, in that order. Since our thoughts go astray so very quickly following an event, and since the only way to correct this is through awareness, the very first stages of perception require close examination.

The brains of animals as well as humans seem to have evolved a method for dealing with emergencies which bypasses fully conscious perception and which is therefore much quicker to initiate action. Once, snorkelling in Jamaican waters, I turned around to see the tail of a large shark. It had quietly swum up behind me and disdainfully rejected me before I even saw it. When I did see it my lightning reaction was to get away. Not the correct reaction but immediate. *Vedanā* had signalled "dangerous" before the slower conscious perception (*sañjanati*) had worked it out. In the same way our body slams the car brakes on in an emergency, after which our thoughts are brought to bear on the matter. I have Parkinson's disease, which slows my conscious movements down, but I can still snatch a falling glass, so I'm very aware of the two mechanisms: lightning *vedanā* followed by slower *saññā*.

Before we look further into the mysteries of *vedanā*, we must consider briefly the hierarchical arrangement of the brain and nervous system. This hierarchical arrangement is so basic in advanced control systems that it applies not only to man but to all animals, not only to all the living beings we know of with nervous systems but to those artificial analogues of the nervous system, neural network computers.

The body-mind evolved as a mechanism for survival. Just like a governmental or business organisation, the system is organised as a hierarchy. If the people at the top had to make every decision the machine would grind to a halt. Therefore all routine and smaller-scale decisions are made at lower levels, leaving the supreme board or cabinet to deal with special cases, chiefly those involving the well-being of the whole organisation. With the human body it is the same. Some processes, such as the digestion and the circulation of the blood, run entirely independently of conscious control. Even the messages directed at the highest centre of the brain, such as those from the eyes, don't run straight there, but pass through several stages of unconscious processing on the way. The processing is aimed at cutting out unwanted data and clarifying the message.

The hierarchical system applies not only to incoming messages but to our responses to them: the complicated body movements we use to get around the world. We don't have to think how to put one leg in front of another. By the time we've learned how to drive a car the lower centres of the brain have become skilled in an amazing repertoire of complicated movements. The acquisition of driving skills is mainly a matter of adding new routines to this repertoire of unconscious programmes. Regular operations such as steering and changing gear, having once been consciously learned, are handed over to a lower level of the hierarchy. On a familiar route even the higher decisions, such as when to change gear, become automatic. "Before rising to any dangerous height, a man ought to know that in emergency his mind and muscles will work by instinct rather than by conscious effort", said Wilbur Wright, inventor with his brother of the aeroplane.

This beautiful system is aimed at keeping the mind clear and ready for important decisions. Unhappily it seldom works like that, because the central mind, with so little left to do, sets off on its habitual wanderings.

Since much of this wandering is also a matter of oft-rehearsed sub-routines, we had better take a look at that too.

Up to this stage we have looked at processes so far down the hierarchy that they are often considered "bodily" skills, since we love to make this spurious distinction between mind and body. Now we go a step up the hierarchy. It is not always realized that our emotions acquire routines almost as readily as the "body" does. These might be called habits rather than skills, and are not always either admirable or useful.

This may seem a far cry from the bare description of *vedanā* in the texts: a painful, neutral or pleasant feeling. But I suggest *vedanā* acts not only in emergencies, when it can be seen to precede *saññā:* it has put a label on most of the objects and incidents in our memory, saying "this is dangerous, this is unpleasant, this is not what I want, this is distasteful", or "this is pleasant, desirable, essential", and so on. Remember that *vedanā* applies equally to the sixth sense, so that it is constantly labelling thoughts as well as external objects as pleasant/unpleasant. Because of this constant uprising of *vedanā* it becomes impossible to disentangle the order of occurrence, so the above analysis may well be wrong. But the order in the Honey-ball of *viññāna* leading through *vedanā* to *saññā* cannot be disputed.

Recognition or perception is a process the first stages of which are unconscious. I have suggested that these unconscious stages take place in *phasso*. An object is sensed and the brain makes an attempt at finding out what it is by looking up a matching image from memory and comparing the two. If they match then recognition has occurred below the level of consciousness and the mind proceeds to *vedanā*. Only after this has occurred can we now consciously say, "That is a tree or a cat or a car, and I do/do not like it". If the match doesn't work out then the brain either goes back to memory for another attempt, or passes the problem to the conscious mind: at which point we say to ourselves "what can that object be?".

Normally all this happens almost instantaneously. Snap! But some-times when the light is low or there is a thick fog we can sense this process as it is happening: We recoil from a vaguely menacing shape, and then start asking: "Is that an animal? Is it moving? It's a log!" Thoughts like these may arise. I have supposed that this unconscious matching up of object with memory happens during *phasso/vedana*. If this is the case, then *sañjanati* (the verb related to *saññā*, the noun) must be the term for consciously recognising or perceiving[42].

It may help to describe a particular incident, a very ordinary one. In the twilight I came onto a large lawn. On the other side was a pile of leaves and small branches, blown off a tree perhaps. But it looked just like one of our cats sitting in a typical posture. This was the perception process going into action. But I happened to catch a glimpse of the mind's reaction. It was not a matter of finding "our cat" in the mind's store of images. For a fraction of a second I saw, not the indeterminate branch, but the whole scene with our cat, tortoiseshell markings and all, where the branch should be. Children seeing faces in the wallpaper go through a similar process. All this must be pre-*vedanā*.

Now we have nearly completed the almost inevitable journey to *papañca*. The scene before our eyes has been unconsciously analysed into separate objects and labelled with all kinds of emotional signals. Now it resides in the conscious mind and arouses thoughts and associations: *vitakka*. But these imaginations go on and on, and this is the essence of *papañca*. The mad mind never stops.

It is quite possible that the five *khandhas* were, at the time of the Buddha, one of the standard classifications of psychology. The Buddha took them one by one and showed them to be illusory. In the deepest sense they are, he said, the five mistakes: five ways of saying "me". I am the body, I feel, I perceive: the "I" is always lodging in one of these illuso-ry abodes.

Once again the paramount point must be made: the Buddha never theorized, never indulged in *ditthi*. All of what he said was for instruction towards practice. His purpose was to point out to us the direction in which lies the ending of *dukkha* so that we can proceed in that direction. Theories are to be put aside, and facts are given only if they will contribute to this end. Everything that the Buddha said should be read in this light.

Our senses tell us that we live in a world of sight and sound and touch. Nevertheless only a tiny proportion of the sensations that bombard us actually initiate the central perception process which the Buddha describes above. I use the term "central" to label that intuitive feeling of one's centre, the seat of this precious consciousness of ours, what I really feel is me. However much this centre may defy analysis, it is so much part of life that it is never questioned by those whom the Buddha called the "ordinary uninstructed worldlings."

Most of the time images may fall in the retina and our ear-drums may vibrate, but nothing has happened so far as our central perception is concerned. Talking to a friend we may remain completely unaware of a nearby conversation (unless our name is mentioned!). An introverted philosopher and a nature lover may emerge from a wood with completely different memories of the last few minutes. Most of the information impinging on us never gains complete entry. It could not be otherwise. Our brains are simply far too small to deal with more than a fraction of the things happening around us.

What have we learnt from the Honey Cake?

Firstly: the fragmentary, discontinuous nature of consciousness. We think of consciousness as one unified entity centred in the head, and now we are told that it is constantly re-arising in one of six different forms. This is an important lesson in *anattā*.

Secondly: the feeling mind acts quicker than the thinking mind. The chain of events leading to *papañca* can be broken at an earlier stage by practising awareness of those rapid responses of like and dislike known as *vedanā*.

Thirdly: In the untrained mind *papañca* inevitably follows conscious thought (*vittaka*). The mind taken over by *papañca* is like a room full of cocktail-party guests struggling to enjoy themselves.

Fourthly, and surely most importantly: the Buddha is talking yet again of a chain of events leading inevitably to suffering. The chain has to be broken somewhere, and the earlier the better. That is why the Buddha emphasizes to Bāhiya, "In the seen there will be just the seen, in the heard just the heard...This itself is the ending of suffering[43]." We continue to sense the world to the full, but once we see clearly the mind taken over by *vedanā* leading to *papañca*, this process looses its power and the fog of ignorance is dispersed.

9
The Story of Māgandiya's Conversion

[From Sutta 75 of the Majjhima Nikāya]

Once the Lord Buddha was lodging with a brahmin named Bhāradvāja, who gave him an honoured place in his fire-shrine room.

Each day the Lord took his bowl to the market-town. After his meal he strode into the forest and sat through the day at the foot of a tree.

One day a mendicant by the name of Māgandiya, a man much given to restlessly roaming around, came to Bhāradvāja's fire-shrine room and saw the place laid out for the Buddha's rest. "It seems to me," he said, "that you have a recluse sleeping here. Who might that be?"

"Māgandiya, this sleeping place is kept ready for the recluse Gotama of the Sākyan clan. Gotama is revered as the perfected fully awakened one, teacher of celestials and men." The Buddha was frequently addressed as Gotama.

"Well", said Māgandiya, "this is a poor sight. It's the sleeping place of Gotama the destroyer of well-being!"

"Mind what you say, Māgandiya. Many wise people – nobles, brahmins, householders and recluses – have great faith in him and in his teaching of skilful action and the Noble Eightfold Path."

"I would like to see your Gotama face to face and tell him that he's just a destroyer of well-being", said Māgandiya.

"If it suits you, Māgandiya, I will tell this to the good Gotama."

"By all means tell him."

Towards evening the Lord Gotama, who had heard this conversation telepathically, ended his solitary meditation and returned to Bhāradvāja's shrine room, to be greeted by Bhāradvāja.

"Did you not have some conversation with the wanderer Māgandiya concerning my sleeping place, Bhāradvāja?"

"This was the very thing I was about to tell you, good Gotama", said Bhāradvāja, greatly startled.

But their conversation was interrupted by the entry of the impatient Māgandiya.

The Lord said to him: "Māgandiya, the eye, the nose, the tongue, the body and the mind all delight in the world around us. But these six senses are guarded and controlled by a Tathāgata, and he teaches how to do this. Is that why you called me repressive?"

"That is so, Gotama," answered Māgandiya.

"What would you say to this, Māgandiya? Suppose that someone who once used to revel in all these enticing, sensual and alluring things that we perceive with our senses, suppose that after a time he came to recognize the arising and passing away of all things, both their sweetness and their danger, and should leave them behind, get rid of his thirst for them, suppress his fever for them, and dwell with a mind inwardly calm. What would you say of him?"

Māgandiya had no answer to this.

"Before I became a homeless one", continued the Buddha, "I enjoyed the pleasures of the senses. I had three palaces, Māgandiya, one for the rainy season, one for the cold weather and one for the hot weather. During the four months of rain I was entertained by female musicians and never left the palace. But after a time I came to know the arising and passing away of sense pleasures and got rid of my craving for them. The mind became inwardly calmed. I saw others burning with this sense-fever and I did not envy them.

"There is a state of joy unconnected with sense-pleasures and with unskilled states of mind, a *deva*-like happiness compared with which ordinary lower pleasures are without delight.

"Māgandiya, let us imagine a rich householder, enjoying the delights of the senses, but of proper behaviour in body, speech and thought. After death he finds himself on a good plane, one of the heaven worlds, in companionship with the *Devas* of the Thirty-three. There in the Nanda Grove, surrounded by nymphs, he experiences the five *deva* senses. Would that young *deva* now envy a rich householder?"

"No! good Gotama, because *deva* sense-pleasures are more wonderful than human sense-pleasures."

"Now, Māgandiya, imagine a leper with his limbs so ravaged and festering, so eaten by vermin, that he tears his open sores with his nails and scorches his body over burning charcoal. Then his friends find a doctor who gives him medicine and cures him so that he can go about freely and at ease. Would that man regret his former leprous state?"

"No, good Gotama. If there is illness then something can be done with medicine. But if there is no illness then medicine can do nothing."

"Māgandiya, supposing that two strong men were to take that cured leper and drag him towards a charcoal fire. Would he not struggle to free himself?"

"Yes, good Gotama. Fire is exceedingly painful!"

"But is fire only painful to him now, or was it also painful in his leprous state?"

"It is painful both now and in his former leprous state. But with his limbs so ravaged and festering, just because of the change in pain he might find fire a relief."

"Even so, Māgandiya, contact with the world through the senses has always been painful. But people so consumed and burning with attachment to sense-pleasures may suppose that a change in the pain will bring relief. This leper, Māgandiya, who scorches his poor body over the burning charcoal only makes his sores the more septic, evil-smelling and putrefying, and there is only a sorry relief from scratching. In the same way a person burning with the fever of the senses gains only a sorry satisfaction in variety."

"Have you ever heard, Māgandiya, of even a king or a chief minister, revelling yet in sense pleasures, who dwells with a mind inwardly calm?"

"No, good Gotama."

"Neither have I, Māgandiya. But all those recluses and brahmins, past, present and future, who come to know the impermanence of sense-pleasures and the stopping of craving, do indeed live without thirst, with minds inwardly calm."

Then the Lord uttered these solemn words:

"Health is the highest possession, *nibbāna* the highest bliss;
And the Eightfold is the Way to security and the deathless."

And the wanderer Māgandiya acknowledged: "Wonderful, good Gotama! These words 'Health is the highest possession, *nibbāna* the highest bliss' are well-spoken. I too have heard that this was said by earlier teachers."

"But what is health and what is *nibbāna*, Māgandiya?"

Māgandiya stroked his limbs with his hands and said, "I am free of disease; I am in good health. This is health, good Gotama, this is *nibbāna*."

"Māgandiya, think of a man blind from birth, who cannot see light or dark, or colours, or the sun, moon and stars. He searches for some pure white unstained cloth because he has heard people say how pleasant a robe made of such material looks. Someone deceptively gives him a greasy grimy robe and he puts it on, crying with pride, 'Now I am wearing unstained white!' If that man blind from birth had known and seen, would he have put on that greasy robe and proudly displayed it? Was it not from confidence in the deceiver that he did it?"

"Indeed, good Gotama, it was from misplaced confidence."

"Even so, others who speak this verse are blind. They do not know health. They do not see *nibbāna*. This whole verse:

'Health is the highest possession, *nibbāna* the highest bliss;

And the Eightfold is the Way to security and the deathless.'

was uttered in the past by perfected fully awakened ones. It has come down gradually to ordinary people. And now you say that health and *nibbāna* refer to this body – a focus for suffering, misery and disease! You have not that noble vision by which you would know health and see *nibbāna*."

"Good Gotama, I rely on your words. Teach me Dhamma that I may know health and see *nibbāna*."

"Māgandiya, supposing that blind man we spoke of goes to a doctor. The doctor gives him the medicine but fails to give him sight. Would not that doctor be very troubled?"

"Yes, good Gotama."

"It would be just so if I were to teach you Dhamma now."

But Māgandiya repeated his supplication.

"Māgandiya, if this blind man were to be cured by the doctor and received vision, would he not cease to have any attachment to his grimy robe, and would he not regard its giver as an enemy, and consider depriving him of life?

"Now if I were to teach you Dhamma so that you could know what is healthy and see *nibbāna*, you would get rid of all attachment to the five *khandhas*, and you would realise that for a long time you had been defrauded and cheated by grasping after *rūpa, vedanā, saññā*, the *sankhāras*, and *viññāna*. You would see that grasping leads to *bhava* (becoming), *bhava* to birth, and birth to old age and dying, grief, sorrow, suffering, lamentation and despair, and that such is the origin of this whole mass of *dukkha*."

"Good Gotama, I rely on you to teach me Dhamma so that I might rise from this seat no longer blind."

"Well then, Māgandiya, you must join the company of true men and listen to the Dhamma. Then you will know for yourself and see for yourself."

"Good Gotama, you have set upright the fallen, you have disclosed what was hidden, you have shown the way to one astray, you have brought a lamp to the darkness. I go to the revered Gotama for refuge, and to the Dhamma and to the Sangha. May I receive ordination in the revered Gotama's presence?"

After the probation period of four months the wanderer Māgandiya received ordination in the Lord's presence. Soon after his ordination the Venerable Māgandiya realized and abided in that matchless goal of the Brahma-farer for the sake of which young men of noble character rightly go forth from home to homelessness.

And he knew:
Destroyed is birth.
Brought to a close is the Brahma-faring.
What was to be done is done.
Being this, being that is no more.
The Venerable Māgandiya had become an *Arahant,* a
Perfected One.

Whereas many *Suttas* are little more than "paste-ups" of block after
block of repetitive material, the *Māgandiya Sutta* stands out for its wealth
of original narrative material and for a surprising criticism of the
Buddha's teaching reminiscent of Freud.

The word *bhunahuno* here translated as "destroyer of well-being" is
obscure (it occurs in neither Rhys Davies' nor Childers' dictionaries),
though it seems to carry overtones of repression (Chalmers), severe rules
(Buddhaghosa) and killer of spiritual growth (Horner).

We need to ask what is most likely to have been Māgandiya's misun-
derstanding? That the Buddha was repressive in the Freudian sense?
There was no doctrine of the subconscious in the Buddha's time.
Repressive in his practice? But he had thoroughly explored asceticism
before rejecting it in order to teach the Middle Way. An over-severe rule
book? The *Vinaya* narrates how the Buddha only made new rules when a
need was demonstrated. A destroyer of development? But spiritual
development is what the Dhamma is all about. Destroyer of well-being?
This depends on what is meant by well-being. We shall see what the
Buddha says about this. Remember that Māgandiya thought he knew all
about the Buddha's teaching.

To find out what Māgandiya was getting at we need to listen carefully to the Buddha's words and Māgandiya's responses.

The Buddha's first approach is to state plainly that however attractive we may find the sensual world, he teaches that the senses should be guarded and controlled. "Is that why you call me a represser?" "Yes," says Māgandiya.

The Buddha then contrasts the life of the hungry sensualist with the realisation that all things are impermanent and that if one can get rid of the feverish thirst for worldly pleasures one's mind becomes calm. To emphasize this message he describes his early life of pleasure and how he came to recognize its worthlessness.

Now comes the revelation that there is happiness beyond happiness, a happiness transcending worldly happiness. To lead Māgandiya onward with something that he will understand the Buddha reminds him of life in the *deva* world after death. Note that this is not proposed as a new belief. It appears to have been a well-known doctrine of the time, and one familiar to Māgandiya, who readily agrees that life in the *deva* world seems vastly preferable.

Next a sombre note is struck. Māgandiya is made to imagine, not a happier situation but one of thoroughly awful worldly pain – advanced leprosy. The leper tries to get away from the pain of his sores by smothering it with another kind of pain, fire.

This is an extreme though unforgettable example. On a smaller scale perhaps most of us can remember biting our fingers or clenching our fist to force the nails into the palm diverting our attention from an acute pain somewhere else, perhaps caused by a dentist's drill.

If a doctor cured the leper would he still try to burn himself? Of course not, says Māgandiya, but then if a person isn't ill in the first place, what's the point of calling a doctor? Māgandiya fails to see the connection between a disease like leprosy and the general condition of suffering in the world: people consumed and burning with attachment.

And now the Buddha solemnly quotes a stanza concerning health and *nibbāna* which Māgandiya claims to have heard. It is very possible that the first line – "Health is the highest possession, *nibbāna* the highest bliss" – was at that time a well known medical saying, *nibbāna* being understood as the ending of a fever. This would explain why it was known to Māgandiya. It was certainly understood by him to refer to the body. But the second line – "And the Eightfold is the Way to security and the deathless" – must surely be the Buddha's. The second line transforms the meaning of the first, which now refers to spiritual health and to *nibbāna* as the calming of the spirit. Following the Buddha's own explanation the whole stanza was understood of old to refer to spiritual well-being, but had through the ages become debased and limited to the medical profession.

Are there signs of exasperation as the Buddha tries yet another approach?

The blind man is deceived into thinking he has acquired the greatest happiness in the shape of a robe which he supposes to be unstained white. In the same way those who suppose that physical well-being is the greatest happiness are blind to the spotless purity of *nibbāna*.

"Now", says the Buddha, "I am the doctor who can cure your blindness."

At last Māgandiya begins to understand what the Buddha is saying and undergoes a conversion which makes him very impatient for further teaching. But the Buddha cautions him. A doctor who administers a medicine before his patient is ready for it may fail to cure him. So Māgandiya must first learn to live as a monk and listen to the Dhamma. Then he will know for himself and see for himself.

Thus Māgandiya learned to see through and therefore exchange the limited and impermanent kind of physical well-being for the indescribably blissful state of *nibbāna*.

10
Aspects of Consciousness

I once dreamt that I was in a museum of jewels. Some cases of jewels were let into the floor. Why were they there? They clearly needed more light to be seen properly[44]. Nowadays, thanks to Freud and his followers we tend to regard the unconscious as a store-house, more or less locked, of past experiences which we don't want to think about, but which, nevertheless have a powerful influence on our actions. The dream told me that there are jewels in the unconscious which can be not only usefully but happily brought to light.

I mention this because talking about consciousness involves the unconscious. The unconscious can simply be thought of as all of the mind's activity that is not conscious. And it is better to call it the "unconscious" rather than the "subconscious" because the term "subconscious" seems to emphasize the lower parts of the mind only. The dream reminded me that the unconscious holds images of wisdom and beauty as well as frightening suppressed experiences.

And we need also to distinguish consciousness from self-consciousness. If we regard consciousness as awareness of the surrounding world, all beings must be conscious merely to survive. Consciousness is consciousness of something. Even the humble bee keeps a flower-map in its tiny mind; as could a computer equipped with suitable sensors. Of course a computer as much in touch with the world as a bee is yet far from realisation.

All advanced control systems use feedback from sensors. Probably in very advanced feedback systems one should not be surprised to find what have come to be called "emergent" (unpredictable) properties. At a very advanced stage of complexity it might well be reasonable to call these properties a rudimentary consciousness.

Self-consciousness, on the other hand, has been defined as "the ability of an individual to perceive their own mental life." Other-consciousness is the other side of the same coin, and implies that we are aware that other beings have feelings like our own. Apparently this faculty is frequently weak or absent in criminals and people who misuse their power. They regard others as no more than cardboard figures to be manipulated.

There are several words in Pali which are never fully explained, or had to await commentators writing several centuries after the Buddha's death. Such words as *khandha, saññā, sankhāra* are consequently difficult to translate, despite massive entries in both Rhys Davies' and Childers' Pali/English Dictionaries. However there is ready agreement that the Pali word *viññāna* should be translated as consciousness.

The cultivation of an ability to pierce through self-illusion (*bhāvanā*) is basic to the Buddhist path. Perhaps we could use the term open consciousness – meaning the apparently hopeless attempt to look at all things within and without as an aware witness. So now, just as we thought things were comfortably tied up and labelled, we had better take a closer look at what the Buddha had to tell us about consciousness.

In the first place it would be a mistake to suppose that the Buddha ever defined his terms as would an academic philosopher. He taught practice, with as little theory as possible. But on one occasion he came close to a definition, and that was the time that he roundly, even harshly, criticized Sāti the Fisherman for spreading a mistaken belief (see Chapter 4). Now Sāti's belief about consciousness would be quite acceptable to most people who think in terms of rebirth, both today and at the time of the Buddha: "It is what speaks and what feels and what experiences the fruits of *kamma*, good and bad." Furthermore he supposes that consciousness is that which continues through life and from life to life. In other words he wants to maintain that there is a continuity of consciousness, or, even if consciousness ceases temporarily, as in deep sleep or between rebirths, he wants that same consciousness to reappear on waking or on rebirth as recognisably the same person.

The Buddha pronounced something so basically different that it needs to be carefully digested. I repeat the relevant passages from Chapter 4:

"Monks, on account of whatever is the origin of **consciousness arising**, by that it is named. If consciousness arises because of an eye and material shapes, then it is known as eye-consciousness. If consciousness arises because of an ear and sounds then it is known as ear-consciousness." And similarly with the other senses, including the sixth sense (which is concerned with the interior world of the mind).

"Monks, on account of whatever is the origin of a **fire burning**, by that it is named. If a fire burns because of wood chips then it is known as a wood-chip fire. A fire made of grass is a grass fire. A fire made of cow-dung is a cow-dung fire, and so on."

The two phenomena are seen as parallel: **fire** and **consciousness.** A bonfire is lit: fire arises. The eye sees a tree: eye-consciousness arises. The fire goes out. Consciousness ceases. Another fire arises elsewhere, feeding this time perhaps on petrol in your car. A bird is singing, and this causes ear-consciousness to arise. And so on . . .

Two points to bear in mind: firstly that consciousness is intermittent; secondly that it has no separate individuality. There are many kinds of fire, but, if anywhere, the individuality is in the things that are burnt, not in the flame. So it is with the "flame" that we call consciousness. It has no individuality, no personality.

There is another and very popular flame analogy:

"But how, Venerable Sir, can rebirth take place without passing over of anything? Please illustrate me this matter."

"If, O King, a man should light a lamp with the light from
another lamp, does in that case the light of the one lamp pass
over to the other lamp?"

"No, Venerable Sir."

"Just so, O King, does rebirth take place without transmigration." [45]

How can the flame carry over any of the characteristics of the previous candle? To me this is not a useful metaphor.

So, if something continues from birth to birth, it is certainly not consciousness. Later commentators, unable to resist a little speculation, have suggested the term *bhavanga* to represent a sort of life continuum. We could ourselves be tempted to describe *bhavanga* as 'psychic genes'. We now understand that our body and mind have been modelled by our parents' genes. But we don't regard these genes as "me". Perhaps a set of non-material "psychic genes" carries essential characteristics to the newly-conceived babe. But, as with the parental genes there is no personality until all this is put together:

"Why do you then harp on the word 'person'? Mara, you are starting from wrong premises. There is nothing but a lot of processes (*sankhāra*); no 'person' is found here. For just as the word 'chariot' is used when its parts are put together, so the word 'person' is commonly used when the five factors (*khandhas*) are present [46]".

The late Ven.Buddhadasa carried this a little further:

A child comes bouncing along and bumps itself on a chair-leg. The child, in anger, hits the chair as hard as he can. The chair has turned into a little soul for that child; the chair has been identified as an individual thing and has been given a personality. And, since that chair aggressively attacked the child, the child strikes back in anger [47].

Rupert Sheldrake has used the analogy of a TV set being examined by aliens unfamiliar with our technology. They are trying to explain the moving pictures. Every item, every connection is exhaustively examined to find where the pictures come from. Of course the possibility of using radio waves, the realisation that the pictures originate far away outside the TV set, cannot be countenanced by these particular aliens. It would be heresy to their basic scientific thinking.

Churning over all these ideas and definitions, we might reasonably conclude that a lot of different *viññānas* or consciousnesses are chasing each other around. We have consciousness as the recognition of the world; self-consciousness for the human's ability to stand back and look at himself/herself as a separate being; open consciousness for the consciousness which is beginning to understand that the boundary between self and the outer world is a construction of the mind, and doesn't correspond with reality. And then we're cut down to size by the Buddha's admonition to Sāti and his fellows, firstly, that there is nothing permanent about consciousness, and, secondly, that individuality and personality are ultimately illusory.

11

A Test of Astrology

On 5 December 1985 an article with the title "A Double-blind Test of Astrology" by Shawn Carlson appeared in the highly respected science journal, *Nature*. A commentary on this test might be of interest to those readers of the *Middle Way* and others who would find it difficult to see the article itself.

In my late 'teens (during the 1940s) I taught myself how to construct astrological charts, but could make no headway with their interpretation. Perhaps this was due to my lack of experience and knowledge of human character. Or was the whole concept flawed? I pondered these questions and thought then that a test of astrology would be easy to plan and that the onus of proof was on the astrologers themselves. Now such a test has been carried out with the close cooperation of three groups of specialists: scientists, astrologers and statisticians.

"So that participating astrologers should be respected by the astrological community, we sought the advice of the National Council for Geocosmic Research, an organisation which has been involved in much astrological research in the past and which has the respect of astrologers world-wide."

The test was in two parts. Both involved matching astrological charts, whose subjects were unknown to the matcher, with personality descriptions in the form of a standard "profile". The personality profile selected was the California Personality Inventory (CPI), chosen over others available "because the advising astrologers judged the CPI attributes to be closest to those discernible by astrology".

Part I of the test went awry. 177 subjects, the majority being college students, all of whose birth dates were known within quarter of an hour, had their astrological charts drawn up but were not shown them. They also filled in the 480 true/false questions of the CPI questionnaire. Of course neither the astrologers nor the CPI assessors met the subjects. Each of one group of subjects was then given his own astrological chart and two other charts chosen at random. He had then to select his own chart. Each of a second group followed the same procedure with three CPI profiles. On this scheme, if only chance operates, a third of the subjects will make the right choice. The result of this Part I trial was that subjects showed no ability to choose their own astrological chart correctly. But they did no better with the CPIs! The author comments: "If subjects cannot recognize accurate descriptions of themselves at a significant level then the experiment would show a null result no matter how well astrology worked". The Part I test, then, was a write-off.

In Part II each participating astrologer was given a birth chart and three CPI profiles, one of which matched the birth chart. The astrologer had to pick the correct CPI profile. Once again chance would make a third of the choices correct. Result: astrologers scored no better than this chance level.

The author summarizes:

"We are now in a position to argue a surprisingly strong case against natal astrology as practised by reputable astrologers. Great pains were taken to insure that the experiment was unbiased and to make sure that astrology was given every reasonable chance to succeed. It failed. Despite the fact that we worked with some of the best astrologers in the country, recommended by the advising astrologers for their expertise in astrology and in their ability to use the CPI, despite the fact that every reasonable suggestion made by the advising astrologers was worked into the experiment, despite the fact that the astrologers approved the design and predicted 50 percent as the 'minimum' effect they would expect to see, astrology failed to perform at a level better than chance. Tested using double-blind methods, the astrologers' predictions proved to be wrong. Their predicted connection between the positions of the planets and other astronomical objects at the time of birth and the personalities of test subjects did not exist."

But this may not be quite the end of the story. One could argue that the CPI, rather than the birth chart, is ineffective in describing character. If so the results would be rendered null, for a 'good' natal chart could not be matched to any CPI if all CPIs were bad. However, having regard for the experience built up in personality testing, I would say that this is not a strong argument.

Gauquelin *(The Scientific Basis of Astrology, 1966)* produced interesting correlations between personality types and the positions of the sun, moon and planets at the times of birth. These were significant enough to attract the attention of that formidable psychologist Eysenck. But the signs of the Zodiac played no part in these correlations, and the significance of the results continues to be debated.

People love putting things and people, into pigeon holes.. We fall all too easily into this trap, even as we try to follow the spiritual instruction to see each person anew. For example, if some guru proposed a personality classification based on trees and assigned people their trees and tree-spirits according to some occult formula, many of us would be going round and saying: "Oh, she's tough, she's an oak tree. He's a bamboo, pliant and tolerant." And it could all be made to seem very plausible.

There is very strong evidence for psychic powers, however weak and unreliable they may often be. Clairvoyants usually require some link with the subject, such as the palm of the hand, or some piece of jewellery constantly worn, or the dregs in an overturned coffee cup – or an astrological chart. This being so the chart itself with the zodiac and the planets, might mean little in itself, but nevertheless could serve as the focus which the clairvoyant requires.

Moreover there may indeed be solar and planetary influences on each one of us which are as yet beyond the reach of present-day astrology.

I cannot do better than end with a wise comment by Trevor Leggett:

"Many people searching for some reality above the ordinary experience of the world tend to think of things of the spirit as a sort of package deal. One may practise Buddhist meditation as a means of attaining spiritual insight and independence, but then one is in duty bound, as it were, also to believe in palmistry (Western and Eastern, though the principles are entirely different), astrology, geomancy, and so on. Apart from the fact that the Buddha himself forbade such practices, there are many disadvantages in the attitude of 'It's all true, and more'. The Chinese saying is that wherever people gather, there the pickpockets too will come, and this is true of spiritual things."

(*Encounters in Yoga and Zen*, p.76)

12
Do You Believe in Belief?

"Nothing is assumed, nothing rejected.
He has washed all beliefs away."
(Sutta Nipāta, stanza 787)

At the dawn of recorded history the Buddha told us not to cling to any belief. But this goes "against the stream" [48], and even Buddhists hang tenaciously onto certain beliefs.

How can we live without belief? For many people this is the negation of religion. People without strongly held beliefs are pictured as characters with no moral code and no compunction to look after anybody but themselves. Such types are, indeed, quite common. Leaders are chosen for their strongly held beliefs.

The largest belief of all, the number one belief is belief in One God. In Christian and Muslim countries this one belief divides the faithful from the infidel. Furthermore to believe in one God is right, but to believe in many gods is wrong.

Some people think the Buddha was an atheist. A glance at the first *Sutta* of the *Majjhima Nikāya* will dispel that notion. To the Buddhist, as to the many sects of India there are exalted and powerful *devas* headed by Brahma, though none lay claim to the power of the Christian and Muslim One God who created the world. The Buddha reminded his listeners that these matters are way beyond our comprehension. Remember the opening words of the *Tao Te Ching*: "The *Tao* that can be spoken of is not the true *Tao*". The ultimate, holy mystery is completely beyond our understanding.

The great Christian and Muslim mystics have used the word God as a focus for their highest experiences, while fully realising the inadequacy of the word. There is a natural bond between Buddhists and such people.

The desire to explain everything is not a new desire, though it has been strengthened by the successes of science. It is as old as mankind. All peoples have had their myths about the creation of the world, about the sun and moon, about whence we came and whither we go. The descendants of these old myths are with us today. In the scientific playground you can take your choice. Perhaps the best myths of the day are those from the astronomers (black holes), the geologists (continental drift), and the palaeontologists (the first woman). They are built on hard-won facts, but nevertheless speculative since there need to be many more facts to fill the gaps in our knowledge.

But it is as well to remember the poisoned arrow story mentioned in Chapter 3. Here the Buddha warned that to spend our time trying to explain our place and purpose in this world is to be like the man shot with a poisoned arrow who, before he would allow any medical treatment, insisted on finding out what kind of a man had shot him, and what kind of bow he used, and other matters of secondary importance. "One thing I teach: the ending of *dukkha*." [27]

It is human nature to seek for links between events, to invent chains of cause and effect. Where witchcraft thrives, all misfortune is caused by witchcraft. The interpretation of omens was once an important part of statecraft. Science has been the great breaker of bogus links and false explanations. But its very success has generated a new intolerance. Materialism has become the new orthodoxy and remains the belief system of most scientists today. True scepticism, the Buddha's scepticism, which neither believes nor rejects, has been forgotten.

Another kind of belief the Buddha warned us against is belief in our own judgement. Many people, particularly in this rather decadent world around us, set great store by their refined taste and aesthetic sense, little realising that they are puppets jerked by the strings of television fashion. However this is of relatively minor importance compared with the thoroughly unhealthy way we judge and criticise each other. Sometimes these judgements lead to acute suffering, but most of the time they are trivial, and go round and round in our heads without ever reaching our mouths. Nevertheless they can generate a background of malaise. What the Buddha wished to convey to us is that our personal likes and dislikes masquerading as judgement must be recognized for the harm they do.

We all find ourselves in situations where we have to make judgements, take sides or choose someone for a job. To be impartial we must learn to distinguish and dissect out as far as possible the ego's heavily disguised commitments.

Two cures are advocated for the disease of idle judgement: one, seeing even close acquaintances anew at each meeting, and, two, watching the sheer absurdity of our prejudices as they actually arise. We will usually discover that it is a low, rather simple part of our mind that originates these judgements, and that they are strongest in our most absent-minded moments. As we study ourselves we sometimes cannot refrain from laughing or crying at our absurdity.

These days there is much talk of "self-fulfilment". The trouble with all efforts at self-fulfilment is that they make people extremely unhappy in trying to pursue happiness. They turn us away from the deepest kind of happiness, or rather a state of serenity deeper than happiness.

Such serenity comes from a very positive acceptance of the situation as it is, and a strong drive to explore, to see into that situation. Note well that this is no matter of putting the lid on emotions and screwing it down. That would probably lead to all the dire consequences described by Freud. On the contrary, emotions are allowed to flower freely in the mind, but are clearly examined as they flower, with detached and fascinated interest. This is the Buddha's practice of *sati*.

Self-fulfilment is not wholly illusory, in the sense that everybody has capacities with the potential for development. We feel contented when we are doing useful and creative work. We feel resentful when blocked from these activities. But the sages are talking about a freedom above and beyond this attachment to self-fulfilment, and we should heed their words.

One could talk about so many kinds of belief. The Buddha's followers must have started inserting beliefs into the scriptures, usually unknowingly, from the moment he died. Even *anattā*, *karma* and rebirth form a sort of background belief for us all, having travelled to the West with the Buddhists. Even these must not be clung to, but held loosely with the knowledge that they are much deeper matters than we at present can understand.

13
Form is Emptiness and Emptiness Form
Rūpaṁ sūnyatā sūnyataiva rūpaṁ [49]

This statement, this paramount mystery, the quintessence of the *Prajñāpāramitā* (Wisdom Books) is quite impossible to understand intellectually. It brings the mind up against a wall with a crash.

Any 19th-century scientist would have been horrified to discover how science today is itself being forced unwillingly into this very same position. Some readers will have seen Stephen Hawking's popular exposition of modern physics, *'A Brief History of Time'*, and they will have assumed that at least Hawking, Einstein and other scientific giants understood what they were talking about. After all, their skilful expositions can give their readers the comfortable impression that they, the readers, also understand in a general kind of way. Much the same kind of manipulation can occur in religious instruction, in honest attempts to explain the evil in God's creation, for example. In fact what scientists understand, or at least what they can manipulate, is the mathematics which underlies all their statements.

The reader may recall observations by Von Neumann and Bertrand Russell (p36) on the mathematical basis of modern physics and how this leads to an impasse in our understanding.

With this in mind we can try to examine some of the infinitesimally small particles that seem to make up our universe.

Most people visualise atoms as tiny billiard balls lined up in neat arrays. Indeed it is now possible to see hugely magnified images of atoms, and they do appear to be like balls packed quite closely together. But that appearance is deceptive. Each atom is composed of a positively charged nucleus around which clouds of electrons circulate. However if we were further to magnify an atom until its nucleus was the size of an orange its electrons would be found orbiting about a kilometre away. In other words, apart from the tiny nucleus and its electrons the atom is composed of empty space.

But we can't stop there. The nucleus itself is said to be composed of quarks, and it is suspected that quarks have zero radius. They are not just small but vanishingly small! At this stage we realize that we have arrived at an untenable position: matter itself is space. And now, to turn this conclusion upside down, quantum physics "involves our regarding individual particles being spread out spatially, rather than always being concentrated at single points." [50] In other words space is matter.

Several other elementary particles are recognized by modern physics. One of these – the neutrino – is apparently produced in large numbers in the interior of the sun as one of the products of the nuclear reactions whereby the sun generates its heat. About 60 billion neutrinos are estimated to pass through each square centimetre of the earth's surface every second – and that includes passing through us.

But we don't feel a thing. Neutrinos can pass right through the earth as if it were not there!

The standard explanation for this is as follows. Any kind of object, whether atom, human body or planet can only feel the presence of other bodies if there is a force between them. The most familiar force is the force of gravity. A second force is the electromagnetic force. There are two others, referred to as the strong force and the weak force. We stand firm instead of flying off into space because the force of gravity pulls the earth and our bodies together. We see things because they emit light rays which interact with our eyes and light rays are electromagnetic. We feel things to be solid because their electromagnetic nature sets up a force field which repels the field in our fingers. This gives us the sensation of touch. An object unaffected by any of the four forces would be totally invisible to us, and not only to us but to any instrument of the physical world that could be devised.

Neutrinos have no electric charge, so they do not feel electro-magnetic force; they have very little mass, if any, so are scarcely influenced by gravity and neither do they interact with the other two forces. This makes them both invisible and impotent to affect anything in our world system, except very occasionally in rare situations.

All this indicates that it is possible for more than one world, each with its own set of forces, to exist in the same space without knowing anything about the others.

To recapitulate. Ever since Mme Curie's discovery of the properties of radium at the turn of the century, science, for all its banishment of old theories and adoption of new ones, has been steadily progressing towards a purely mathematical description of the world. This mathematical description cannot be translated into words; that is to say it makes no intellectual sense.

It would surely be a mistake to suppose that Buddhist sages in the past already understood the physical world in a mathematical or even an intellectual sense. Rather they arrived at the same paradox through spiritual practice.

The idea that many worlds co-exist in the same space is not new. It was in the mind of primitive man. However, instead of speculating on exotic possibilities such as clairvoyance and telepathy we would be wise to turn back to the Heart Sutra and the statement which is the title of this article.

The message is clear: whether scientist or aspiring Buddhist, we do not, indeed cannot, see the world as it really is. Yet we cling to our illusion. Therefore we suffer.

14
The Karma Buck Stops Here

You may recall that President Harry Truman had a notice on his desk that became famous: "The buck stops here." He was, of course, referring to the fact that the U.S. President ultimately takes responsibility for all major decisions, and blame for all major disasters.

Recently I have become increasingly aware of how our actions and thoughts are creating *karmic* fruits on the spot, in real time as a computer programmer might say. (Computing in real time means that data are dealt with on the spot, instead of being accumulated for later analysis.)

An imaginary but common scenario: two people are quarrelling. Each untrue criticism or phrase meant to hurt, or distortion of the truth, loads *karmic* results on the aggressor. In the standard "argument game" each hurtful statement gets an even more hurtful response, and so the situation escalates, either to violence or until one party gives in. Or both go away, perhaps to work out their anger in some other way, very likely on some other person.

Today the usual advice is: get it all out of your system, don't bottle it up, make your complaints known, assert your rights. For many people this might indeed be the best advice, perhaps for most people. But sooner or later we all have to grow up, to reconsider that standard "let it all hang-out". Mind you, it's important to pick out the good part of this form of advise: don't bottle it up.

But at that point we should bear in mind the Buddha's road to the ending of suffering, which he called *sati:* in all situations be as often as possible aware of what's going on in the inner world of the mind, be the witness watching the body/mind grapple with anger, fear and hopelessness. And don't be resistant to turning the other cheek, Jesus's great teaching. This overturned the old orthodox command, "an eye for an eye and a tooth for a tooth". It might be objected that the world would turn upside down if we all followed this path. Hopefully it will indeed turn upside down in some distant future, when people have stopped clinging to their imagined rights.

As an experiment, next time you have a criticism to make, monitor the situation carefully. The common routine starts with your feeling a little irritated about someone, and anxious to find an opportunity for confrontation, to get it over with. You find the opportunity. You make your complaint, and it is accepted, often reluctantly. Now that it's over, do you feel happier than before? After all the job's done. And how about the other person? Does she or he feel happier than before?

Commonly neither party feels happier! Indeed the seed of long-lasting enmity may have been sown. So the experiment goes as follows.

(This is one situation where forward planning is essential.) Your objective becomes that at the end of the exchange both sides should feel happier, and you plan the confrontation in accordance with this objective. Obviously ego-centred complaints like "you're not giving me what I want" are doomed from the start. But with necessary criticism, however carefully and hopefully you plan, it doesn't always work, even when you are full of good will. Nevertheless it really is worth making the effort.

The popular assumption is that each person has real or imagined "rights", which sometimes have to be fought for. All of us can indeed be wronged. But what should we do about it? We assume that we'll be walked over unless we defend ourselves or retaliate. Indeed we often are walked over. So be it! At the same time one has to acknowledge a threshold of violence, of maltreatment, of rape, of torture, perpetrated on self, friends or family. Beyond this threshold we, in our imperfection, will not be able to maintain "right purpose" – non-violence. So be it. We have at least to acknowledge this awful fact.

To return to everyday confrontations, which can be vicious enough: is remaining silent the only way out? Silence may be filled with pain and destructive thoughts. Something much better, something much more constructive, than just silence is needed. Silence in this situation doesn't mend anything, and can make one partner appear odiously pious and the other trapped in anger. Each situation is different. There's no standard way out. *Sati*, accompanied by compassion, together with some hard thinking, can produce good results – sometimes. Not always.

On the positive side, it seems one can, initially in a small way, at all times of the day, put oneself aside, leaving the stage clear, the river banks clean, for the divine wisdom/compassion to flow through the meditator and round us all – not just round the meditator. This is very much offering yourself as a channel for the divine. There's no question of a personal bonus, nothing particularly in it for you personally.

The *karma* buck also operates in physical illness. When they're ill, most people who pray ask for a cure. It is only sensible to accept what medical treatment is available. But beyond that, however tempting, our prayer should be for help to face up to our illness and to learn what we can from it. Conversely, on hearing of other peoples' suffering, those who have a background belief in *karma* (Hindus as well as Buddhists) have been known to remain passive in the face of suffering – to state that the sufferers are now working off some fruits of past *karma*, and that it would therefore be unhelpful to interfere. But the practice of mindfulness generates compassion for all, and demonstrates the invalidity and unhealthiness of this attitude.

It may seem that the exercise of *sati* just described is small stuff, seeming possibly trivial in times of acute pain and loss. This is certainly true at the beginning, but it can be that first step in the thousand-mile journey.

Stop passing the Karma Buck! Then we can cheerfully recall that, as Nisarga Datta says, "When you are no longer attached to anything, you have done your share. The rest will be done for you" [51].

15
The World a Dream?

H omage to the Blessed One, the Perfect One, the Fully Awakened One.

Why Fully Awakened? Is it that we are all asleep and in a dream?

I can remember the awe I felt on first studying the "Discourse on the Root of Things" (the *Mūlapariyāya Sutta*). This is the first *sutta* of the *Majjhima Nikāya*, the collection of "middle-length" *suttas* of the Pali Canon.

But this *sutta* is a difficult one, at any rate in translation.

I will be bold enough to summarize it thus:

The "uninstructed worldling" imagines the earth and all beings in relation to "me", and cannot imagine otherwise. By contrast one who has become an *Arahant*, who has done what was to be done, whose fetters have been utterly worn away, he knows the world deeply, and he does not imagine it in relation to "me".

Let me try to state this in different terms: that we see everything from one point of view; that, without thinking, we each regard ourselves as being in the centre of things.

All this introduces distortion into the understanding of our surroundings. This is intellectually obvious, and from time to time we might make quite big efforts to be impartial, to correct this fiercely-defended prejudice. After all, out there in the outside world is a huge body of knowledge which everyone agrees about. The sun rises and sets, you can't see in the dark, seeds become flowers. And so on. We all agree about these things, and we wouldn't agree if we each of us saw the world in a wholly different, wholly personal way.

But we differ widely in matters which affect the ego directly in pleasure or pain, such as who is nice and who is nasty, what is enjoyable and what is harmful. Here the differences can be striking. But even this hardly touches what the Buddha meant on how the emotions and the intellect have built this castle of the ego, fortified to resist pain, and to allow entry only to those things we imagine will give us maximum pleasure.

Now we usually regard most of the world of the senses as not part of "me", except of course "my" body. Other things may belong to me, feel almost part of me, like an old coat. But most are definitely "not me". With the mental world of the sixth sense it is the other way round. All of it appears to be "me" or "mine". But perhaps this is all part of the illusion. Perhaps the outside world and the inside world are equally "me" – or equally "not me"! After all we now know a little about how the brain unconsciously selects and processes all those myriad of messages that arrive via the senses. What we see is not the world about us but the brain's interpretation of it[42].

The Buddha required each of us to find things out for ourselves. He therefore gave us a practice. This practice is set out in one of the great documents of the world: the *Satipatthāna Sutta* (Chapter 1)

As we have seen, in this *sutta* the Buddha teaches us how to be aware of the body, of the pleasure/pain feelings, and of mental happenings. We are to sit quietly attentive, watching the body or watching the mind, clinging to nothing, particularly not clinging to our favourite beliefs. The mind becomes quiet. We become a witness who observes without interfering, but very attentively. We watch the rise and fall, the coming into being and passing away, of breath and thoughts.

What do we conclude? That can only be discovered in actual practice. But of course the answer has been given all over the place, in all good works on meditation. The watcher comes to understand that what can be observed – in the body – in the mind – cannot be the observer because they are the observed. They cannot be me because they are being watched by me! The quieter the mind becomes the more subtle the observation, the more the very depths of the personality are seen to be not-me. But always the mystery of I the watcher remains. The Buddha turned aside all attempts to penetrate this mystery, knowing that it is beyond the powers of the intellect.

Now let us see what usually happens. We have already been brainwashed by teachers with the best intentions into trying to believe that "I do not exist". Success in this form of Buddhism appears to hang on my being able to believe in my non-existence! So, instead of quietly observing without holding any opinions on the matter, we sit and try to persuade ourselves into the opinion that our ego is disappearing, and, with some more effort along the same lines, will be persuaded to disappear altogether. Can't we live with a mystery that actually gets deeper the more we penetrate it? Can't we be content to be the quiet witness full of wonder?

Perhaps the outside world and the inside world are two aspects of one world. Perhaps the body-and-mind which I regard as myself is but a small element woven into a marvellous and intricate pattern. One thing is clear: the unaided intellect is quite unable to step out of egocentricity, and therefore quite unable to experience this pattern of things. You may take a degree in philosophy. I hope you don't, because it won't get you any nearer to the truth.

It is certainly very difficult, possible nevertheless after much meditation, to look at ourselves/the world without forming beliefs or opinions. Yet this is what the Buddha told us most insistently must be done. Remember the stanza from the *Sutta Nipāta* at the head of Chapter 12.

Most of us have taken some hard knocks in the matter of love for another which is not reciprocated. Such love of a particular person always has an element of clinging, whether between woman and man, or parent and child. If we don't get what we want in love returned, such love, especially sexual love, can undergo a chameleon-like change to hatred and much pain. It's all very well in such situations to call up our reserves of *mudita,* the Buddha's word for being glad at another's happiness. Our pain seems as if it's going to continue for ever. All this is a result of clinging. And we cling because we are deluded about the nature of this world.

"The 'world' is purely perceptual and it has neither more nor less factual location when perceived in a waking state than when perceived in a dream."   (Wei Wu Wei)

If the world is a dream, then why bother about wisdom and compassion? The answer is: don't try to cultivate them. They arise naturally as clinging ends.

Sometimes we "wake up" in a dream. We realize we're dreaming and suddenly see things very clearly and distinctly. The experience is of heightened consciousness and very exhilarating. Perhaps some equivalent waking-up has also to occur in the "real" world.

Chuang Tzu's little riddle is well known [52].

He dreamed he was a butterfly. "And now", he asks, "Am I a man who dreamed he was a butterfly or a butterfly dreaming he is a man?"

But it is evident that, in spite of Wei Wu Wei and Chuang Tzu, the world is not just a dream world such as we dream every night. Every night our dreams are different. But the world continues, at any rate for a very much longer time than the longest dream. The sun rises and sets reliably day after day. And the old philosophical question, "If I am dreaming, are you all just parts of my dream or am I just a part of yours?" goes unanswered.

Neurologists have pointed out that the brain carries on working irrespective of whether there is any sensory input or not. Thus waking consciousness is dreaming – but dreaming constrained by external 'reality' [53].

There is something much deeper which we, as individuals, with our noisy minds, cannot grasp.

Why do we find it so difficult to give up these limiting ego-notions? That at least we can partly understand. They are the habit of many, many lifetimes. The successful practice of the Dhamma entails a revolution – in the words of Krishnamurti: "the only true revolution."

And so we continue our earnest contemplation of the mystery.

16

The Perennial Practice

In 1946 Aldous Huxley published an influential little book, *The Perennial Philosophy*. He used the word "philosophy" in its original and literal sense: love of wisdom. It is the love of wisdom which inspires our practice of the Buddha's teaching. And so a perennial love is nurtured by a perennial practice.

By the phrase perennial practice we need to emphasize two things. First, as we well know, the Buddha taught a practice not a creed, a practice by which we come to see for ourselves: "Monks, do you not speak that which is known by yourselves, seen by yourselves, found by yourselves?"[54]. Second, the teaching is perennial in the grandest sense: it belongs to no particular place or age; it is here with us now, it always has been and it always will be. The Buddha did not claim to be the first, rather a renewer. Nevertheless the *Satipatthāna Sutta,* in which he laid out the practice clearly and simply, is the oldest document that exists where that has been done. How could any document in the history of the world be more important? Yet this sutta is no more than a string of words until translated into practice (See Chapter 1).

And now comes the question of aim. If I take up meditation, what will it do for me? What will I get out of it? As things are I'm wandering around aimlessly right now, so don't tell me it's aimless!

If we declare we have no aim in meditating, psychiatrists will be quick to provide one, and it may not be flattering. We certainly start with an aim, and the closer it is to the "ending of suffering" the better. In actual fact those who come to meditation and stay with it simply have a feeling of coming home. There is no need of an aim.

Perhaps that's all we should say on aims. Unfortunately many shallow detrimental answers have been put around. Meditation will make you more successful at work. Meditation will bring you blissful experiences (sometimes, but not necessarily true). Meditation, it is whispered, will confer psychic powers. It is not surprising that some people come to meditation with freaky ideas of what it will do and what it is for.

Another notion that has got around is that the simple practice outlined in the *Satipatthāna Sutta* is no more than the first step in a series of initiations, of increasing privilege and secrecy, conferring knowledge and power. Other techniques and styles and schools there certainly are, some of them excellent. But it's sad to see anybody changing around for the wrong motives or simply from lack of perseverance. The practice the Buddha taught is complete in itself.

Sooner or later we realise that the mind is in a fever and that meditation is the cure to that fever; that the mind is a prison and meditation is, not the unlocking of the door, but the realisation than the prison is an illusion.

The keyword is simplicity. Shunryu Suzuki wrote just one book, but a jewel of a book: *"Zen Mind, Beginner's Mind"*. Our ignorance is so breathtaking and the practice so simple that we, the egos, are always ignorant beginners. We are ignorant of this moment. This moment is what we become aware of. We dive into the universe of this moment simply by stilling the mind.

I have tried to assist the meditator by selecting articles on practice in this book. So, to end, here are a few quotations from works of spiritual knowledge. There is no need to make a distinction between God and the blessed unknowable.

> In a forest or under a tree or in an empty place, one sits down cross-legged, back erect, and arouses awareness. Aware, one breathes in; aware one breathes out. . . And so one fares along, independent, clinging to nothing in the world. . . awareness is established precisely to the extent necessary for bare attention.
>
> (*Satipatthāna Sutta*)

> Then he entirely recognizes that he has no right to say "I" or "mine". At this stage he beholds his helplessness: desires fall away from him and he becomes free and calm. He wishes that which God wishes: his own wishes are gone.
>
> (Abu Sa'id, Sufi)

> . . .this means being prepared to loose contact with every article of faith that had previously sustained one in one's spiritual life.
>
> Martin Israel (Anglican), "Smouldering Fire", p.170

You need not know what you are. Enough to know what you are not. What you are you will never know, for every discovery reveals new dimensions to conquer.

Nisarga Datta (Vedanta)," I am That", Bk.II,p.126)

Openness is all – openness to the play of existence, whether it is manifest as God, as man, as animals or the world of nature.

Aelred Graham (Roman Catholic)

The entire consciousness must be still, not wanting, not seeking and never pursuing. The totality of consciousness must be still and only then, that which has no beginning and no end can come into being. Meditation is the emptying of consciousness, not to receive, but to be empty of all endeavour. There must be space for stillness.

Krishnamurti[55]

EPILOGUE

Remember the story of the devil walking one evening with a friend? Someone ahead of them stoops to pick up an object that has caught his eye. "What's that?", asks his friend. "It's a bit of truth", replies the devil. "That's bad news for you!" says his friend.

"Not a bit of it", laughs the devil, "Just wait. In a moment he will start to formulate it."

The Dhamma knows no boundaries. To emphasize its universality, here is a quotation from a remarkable Hindu sage. But one could find the message in any mystical tradition, whether Christian, Jewish or Islamic[56].

"Question: How are the paths of *jhana* (wisdom) and *bhakti* (devotion) related to each other?

Mother Meera: To be a *jhani* is to know, and the more that you know the Divine, the more you love. To be a *bhakti* is to choose the path of love, and the more you love the Divine, the more you know."

At the end of the day it would be natural for the reader to ask, "why call yourself a Buddhist. why not a Christian or Sufi mystic or one of the many Hindu paths?"

GLOSSARY

(Without going into details. It is useful to know that 'c' is pronounced 'ch' as in 'church'. 'ṁ' with a dot over it reads '-ng')

akusala
(see *kusala*)

anattā
Usually regarded as a Buddhist doctrine: there is no permanent self. More properly it was the Buddha's term for the practice of examining the internal world to discover what is not self.

Arahant
One who has attained the highest: *Nibbāna*.

avijjā
Spiritual ignorance, lack of higher knowledge.

bhava
Becoming, rebirth, attachment to *samsara*(the world)

bhavana
Developing the mind

bhavanga
A term which later writers have used for the life continuum, that which is reborn.(see ch.10)

citta

Heart/mind. In the West we talk about the heart meaning the emotions,and the mind meaning the operations of reason. But this separation doesn't work very well in reality. The heart gives reasons for its actions, the mind cannot reason without being swayed by emotions. Maybe it is not useful to seperate them. To study *citta*, turn to the 3rd foundation of *satipatthāna* (Ch.1).

deva

A celestial being, an angel. In Asia there is a general background belief in spirits of all kinds and that there is a *Deva* realm, where virtuous people go after death. This is all quite likely to be true, and the Buddha didn't question it. But it remains outside our present comprehension.

Dhamma

The word Dhamma (Sanskrit *dharma*) has evolved from the earliest Vedas of the Brahmins, perhaps as long ago as 2500 BC. Dhamma was the Universal Law, in the widest possible sense, and applied to all sentient beings including, of course, humanity. The way things are – or ought to be.

In keeping with "the way things are", the Buddha used Dhamma when he needed a term with the widest possible sense: "All Dhammas are without self". " There is nothing in the universe or outside, good or bad, conditioned or unconditioned, relative or absolute, which is not included in this term." (Walpola Sri Rahula, "What the Buddha Taught", Fraser (1982), p.38)

Since the whole of the phenomenal world is perceived through our senses, Dhamma on other occasions takes on a narrower meaning:the inner world, the objects of our imagination.

Lastly, in an easy transition, Dhamma, in the hands of the Buddhists, became the Teaching of the Buddha, which is about the way things are or

should be. In this book that is how it will be used, unless otherwise stat-
ed.

dukkha

Suffering in all its ramifications. There is a tendency among Western
teachers, faced with a relatively prosperous audience, to play *dukkha*
down and translate it as a weak "unsatisfactoriness".
This will not do! On those occasions when we find ourselves comfortable,
images from the TV screen crowd into our consciousness to remind us of
the truly appalling suffering among the world's refugees and the world's
starving. And, even in the comfortable areas of the world, people suffer
dreadfully from desire and jealousy.

indriya

Originally the term meant "belonging to the god Indra". Under
Buddhism, in its fivefold form it gathers together those mental qualities
essential to followers of the Dhamma: *saddhā* (confidence), *viriya* (energy),
sati (awareness), *samādhi* (concentration), *paññā*(wisdom).

kamma

Since the Sanskrit term *karma* has become so familiar to Western readers I
have sometimes used it instead of the Pali form *kamma*. Literally "action".
Good *karma* results in good effects, and vice versa. It has to be empha-
sised that *karma* must not be used in the framework of a God who deals
out reward and punishment. *Karma* is a natural law. The effect of *kamma*,
its fruit, is called *kamma vipāka*.

kāya

The physical body: "This my body is material made up from the four great
elements, born of mother and father, fed on rice and gruel, impermanent,

liable to be injured and scraped, broken and destroyed." (*Digha, sutta* 2, para 83). Compare *rūpa*.

khandhas

The standard translation of the five *khandhas* or elements of a person: *rūpa* (material forming the body), *vedanā* (feelings), *saññā* (perception), *sankhāras* (mental formations)), and *viññāna* (consciousness). The *sankhāras* seem never to have been closely defined until the *Abhidhamma Pitaka*, which may have ventured far from the Buddha's usage of the terms, so their meaning remains obscure. The *khandhas* are in no sense vital to the *dhamma*. For all we know they may have been the standard anaiysis of a person before the Buddha's teaching.

kusala

Healthy, wholesome, skilful. *akusala* is the opposite.

mudita

One of the four *brahma-vihāras,* or divine abidings: *mettā* (loving-kindness), *karuna* (compassion), *mudita* (sympathetic joy) and *upekhā* (equanimity). *Mudita,* meaning to be glad at another's good fortune, is not always easy when the other is an opponent.

nāmarūpa

The meeting of the immaterial (*nāma*) and the material (*rūpa*) parts of the person.

nibbāna

Here, as with *karma*, the Sanskrit form, *nirvāna,* is more familiar. A goal which, until one attains it, is quite impossible to describe. And for those few who have, words are apparently useless. All that can be done is to answer every attempt at explanation with "Not this! Not this!"

papañcā and *papañcā-saññā-sankha*
Following Bhikkhu Ñanananda, whose booklet "Concept and Reality" (Buddhist Publication Society, Sri Lanka.1971) gives the definitive translation and discussion on these two terms, *papañcā* describes the ever present mental turmoil as like a monkey leaping from branch to branch, grabbing a fruit here, dropped, another fruit likewise, never stopping. The longer phrase emphasizes further involvement in the basic mental noise.

paticca samuppāda
The wheel of life. Interdependant origination. Conditioned genesis.
The 12 factors can be said to follow each other in a chain, or on the wheel of *saṁsāra*. The 12 spokes of the wheel are:
avijjā (spiritual ignorance), *sankhāras* (see *khandhas*), *viññāna* (consciousness), *nāmarūpa* (see above), the six senses, *phasso* (contact), *vedanā* (feelings), *tanhā* (thirst), *upādāna* (clinging), *bhava* (becoming), *jāti* (birth), decay/pain/decay/death.

phasso
Contact. The first stage in the process of perception. See ch.8.

rūpa
Walshe (Thus Have I Heard, note 337): "Both *rūpa* and *kāya* can on occasion be translated as 'body', but there is a difference. *Rūpa* is body as material, especially visible, form, while *kāya* is body as aggregate, as in 'a body of material, a body of men'."

samādhi
Concentration, but not the intense activity which, for example, the scientist brings to bear on a research problem. The simplest form of *samādhi* is *ānāpānasati*, concentration on the breath, but there are many aids, such as

concentrating on a pattern or *rūpa*. The practice of *samādhi* is said to lead to the *jhānic* states, which have been described as delightful spiritual food.

sammā ditthi
Right views. The first heading of the Noble Eight-fold Path. Buddhists sometimes get into quite a twist in trying to reconcile 'Right views' with 'No views'. 'Right views' seems as if we are allowed views/beliefs, provided they are the right ones! Perhaps the best way out is to translate as 'Right understanding', meaning right understanding of the Dhamma as practice.

saṁsara
Cycle of continuity, rebirths.

sangha
The community of Buddhist monks.

sañ jānāti
He perceives. The verb from of *sañña (see below)*.

sankhāras
Usually translated as 'mental formations'. See under *khandhas* for a note on this deliberately vague rendering.

saññā
Usually translated as 'perception'. See ch.8.

sati
Awareness, mindfulness. The *Satipatthāna Sutta (Dīgha Nikāya, sutta 22; and Majjhima Nikāya, sutta 10)*is centred on this word.

tanhā

Thirst, craving, hunger (for life experiences).

vedanā

Feeling. The second Foundation of Awareness in the *Satipatthāna*

viññāna

Consciousness. See ch.8.

vipāka

The fruit or result of *karma*.

vipassanā

In the Theravada there are two great meditative roads: *samathā* and *vipas-sanā*. The former uses concentration techniques. The latter, *vipassanā*, choiceless awareness, allows simple acknowledgement, without praise or blame, of the things that float into consciousness, but never lets them carry you away.

A NOTE ON REFERENCES TO THE PALI CANON

The Pali Canon, the basic scriptures of Theravada Buddhism, are divided into three "baskets", the *Tipitaka:*
Vinaya Pitaka – Sutta Pitaka – Abhidhamma Pitaka
  Discipline – Teaching – Philosophy
  The references in this book are all to the *Sutta Pitaka*, which is in its turn subdivided into five collections (*Nikāya*):

Digha Nikāya	Long Discourses
Majjhima Nikāya	Middle Length Sayings
Saṁyutta Nikāya	Kindred Sayings
Anguttara Nikāya	Gradual Sayings
Khuddaka Nikāya	Small Books

Reference to any of the suttas, or discourses, in the *Dīgha* and the *Majjhima Nikāyas* is straightforward, since in both cases the *suttas* are numbered straight through from beginning to end. Thus the *sutta* or discourse "To Prince Bodhi" can be referred to as *Majjhima Nikāya sutta* 85, or if a particular passage is required, one could give the page number either of the English translation by the Pali Text Society ("Middle Length Sayings", vol.3, p.279), or of the Pali text (*Majjhima Nikāya*, vol.2, p.91)

The *Saṁyutta* is further subdivided into five *vaggas*, each of which is a separate collection of *suttas*, beginning at number 1.

The *Anguttara* is less straightforward: 11 *nipātas* divided into a number of *vaggas*, each of which contain 10 or more *suttas*.

The easiest way to study any part of the *Khuddaka* is to regard it as a collection of separate works. Thus the *Dhammapada*, the *Udāna* and the *Sutta*

Nipāta are all part of the *Khuddaka*. The *Sutta Nipāta* is arranged into 1149 stanzas.

For any serious study of the Pali Canon, one of the Wheel publications, "An Analysis of the Pali Canon" (ed. Russell Webb), Buddhist Publication Society, PO Box 61, Kandy, Sri Lanka, is to be recommended.

Notes and References

1   NYANAPONIKA THERA, "The Heart of Buddhist Meditation", Rider, London. A full translation of the Satipatthana Sutta, with many other relevant quotations.

2   WALSHE, MAURICE, "Thus Have I Heard," A translation of the "Long Discourses of the Buddha" (the *Digha Nikaya*), Wisdom, London (1987). The *Satipatthana Sutta* is *Sutta* 22.

3   VEN.PHRA KHANTIPALO, "The Young Buddhist", Singapore (1982), pp.115-9.

4   The *Sutta* appears twice in the Pali Canon: as *Sutta* 22 of the *Digha Nikāya*; and, word for word the same, but without verses 18 to 21, as *Sutta* 10 of the *Majjhima Nikāya*.

For a good and complete translation, I suggest Maurice Walshe's translation of the *Dīgha Nikaya*,(published as "Thus Have I Heard" by Wisdom,London(1987) or Nyanaponika Thera's "Heart of Buddhist

Meditation", Rider, London(1969). Incidentally "Thus Have I Heard"should be recommended, not only as the best introduction that I know to the Theravada Canon itself, but as a mine of information in its references.

5   Recalling the Buddhist emphasis on no belief, this statement, "the only way" seems highly dogmatic. But we must recall that this is a statement of practice, the practice of inner stillness common to all mystical traditions.

6   The practice is to watch the body as it is (small movements, aches and pains), not to overlay the watching with thoughts and imaginations.

7   There is to be no attempt at controlling the breath.

8   Some readers may have seen the early forms of wood-lathes, pole-lathes, which do not give continuous rotation. A cord is attached to a springy wooden pole at a high point. It is passed once round the spindle and down to a foot pedal. The cutting tool is applied to the work as the turner presses on the pedal. The cutting tool is then raised from the work as the pole pulls upwards.

9   Internally and externally: this is usually interpreted as watching the meditator's body and watching someone else's body, but watching someone else's body seems to plays no part in practice today. Perhaps some explanation has gone missing.

10   This beautiful statement carries great weight.

11   All these actions are mentioned in order to ram home the point that there should be no let-up in the watching. Achaan Cha has said, "Some people think that the longer you sit the wiser you must be. I've seen chickens sit on their nests for days on end. Wisdom comes from being mindful in all postures. Your practice should begin as you awaken in the morning. It should continue until you fall asleep."

12   One of the achievements of progress from the time of the Buddha to today is that biological and medical studies have shown us the fantastic internal beauty of the human body. Without this knowledge the organs do indeed seem to be repulsive. At any rate the Buddha, having enumerated the main contents of the body, uses a metaphor which compares the body to the neutral, disinterested sorting of rice and beans in a provision bag.

13   This simile as it stands seems not to help in any discernible way. Walshe calls it "an unpleasant image".

14   These charnel-house contemplations have the purpose of overcoming rather than generating disgust. The lesson, of course, is impermanence.

15   *Vedanā* is discussed more fully in ch.8. Suffice it to state that it refers to the first impression we get through the senses, the first lightning response just conferring a label: pleasant/unpleasant/neutral. It should not be confused with *citta* (note 16).

16   *Citta.* In the West we are accustomed to refer emotional matters to the heart and rational matters to the mind, as if the two can be separated. *Citta* refers to the whole mental state: heart/mind. It is perhaps best translated as "mood". The practice here is to become aware of the "set" of the

mind which is often slow to change; for example whether elated or depressed. This is quite different to the lightning response of *vedanā*.
If we think of *vedanā* as waves breaking on the shores of consciousness, then *citta* is the state of the ocean at that time.

  What drives people to elation or depression? Circumstances certainly are a factor, but only a factor. Plenty of rich people living in luxury have attempted suicide. Plenty of the very poor, or those in deep pain seem to have their moments of joy. With the development of mood-changing drugs depression can often be cured, or at least held at bay. Two hundred years ago few would have guessed how dependent on the chemical balances in the brain is mood or is very definitely "not me".

17   Dhamma.The reader should refer to the Glossary on Dhamma. Scholars agree that dhamma is here used in the sense of "mental objects". And I think that all who have practised *Satipatthāna* would agree that the division into *kāya, vedanā, citta* and Dhamma covers the situation neatly where, having meditated on body(*kāya*), feelings(*vedanā*) and mind-set (*citta*), we turn to the fourth Dhamma meditation of letting thoughts arise and pass away without grabbing hold of them. This is called *vipassanā*. Krishnamurti talked of "choiceless awareness". But the text under Dhamma follows a different course. It reminds one of airline pilots tirelessly checking all controls and indicators as the flight proceeds. It seems as if in the remote past some transcriber of this *Sutta* understood the word dhamma to have here been used in its other sense: the Buddha's Teaching, so he thought it would be helpful to slip in here a summary of the Teaching.

18   The *Sutta* under discussion is often referred to as the *Kālāma Sutta*, since the Kālāmas were the centre of attention. In fact the correct title is Those of Kesaputta, and it is to be found in the Pali Text Society "Book of Gradual Sayings", Vol.I(1960), p.170. Pali Reference: *Anguttara-Nikāya*,III,

*Tika-Nipāta,*VII *Mahāvagga,* section 65. (One could hardly imagine a more convoluted reference!)

19   VEN. PHRA KHANTIPALO, "An Interpretation of the Kalama Sutta", in "The Young Buddhist" (1982), Singapore Buddha-Yana Organisation, pp.115-119.

20   See also Middle Length Sayings,vol.I, p.321.

21   "Seeing the danger of such miracles, I dislike, reject and despise them." *Digha Nikaya* ("Thus Have I Heard", "The Long Discourses"), *sutta* 11, para.5.   I think it would be correct to say that the Buddha came to despise psychic powers from his own very extensive experience of how they could be misused.

22   *Dīgha-Nikāya, sutta* 14. The lengths of *kappas* varies, but are usually in excess of half a million years. Probably this passage is inserted to emphasize the antiquity of the Dhamma.

23   *Saṁyutta-Nikāya,* XIV,10

24   SRI NISARGADATTA MAHARAJ, "I Am That", Chetana, Bombay (1981)vol.II, p.126

25   *Majjhima-Nikāya,* Pali Text Society,Vol.1, *Sutta* 22. "Middle Length Sayings", Pali Text Society, Vol.1, p.173

26   *Majjhima-Nikāya, suttas* 26 & 85.

27   *Majjhima-Nikāya, sutta* 63.

28   See the first *sutta* of the *Majjhima-Nikāya*.

29   BLOFELD,JOHN, Compassion Yoga, p.27.

30   The name, Sā ti, joyful, is quite different to *sati*, awareness.

31   " Kindred Sayings", Pali Text Soc., chap.XXXV,28

32   *Saṁyutta-Nikāya,,* IV, p.400.

33   *Saṁyutta-Nikāya* II,114

34   *Ñānananda*, "The Magic of the Mind", p.25

35   SHELDRAKE, RUPERT, "A New Science of Life", Blond & Briggs,1981).

36   BERTRAND RUSSEL quoted by Koestler, "Roots of Coincidence", p.99.

37   *Saṁyutta-Nikāya*, I,135

38   *Majjhima Nikāya*, Sutta 38.

39   *Anguttara-Nikāya*, VI,118.

40   ÑANANANDA, "Concept and Reality", Buddhist Publication Society, Kandy, Sri Lanka (1971).

41   It is natural for the student of Buddhism to demand clear-cut definitions of such words as *saññā* and *viññāna*. Later commentators have indeed attempted such definitions. But, just as most people today remain

vague about 'perception' and 'consciousness' whereas philosophers define them to suit their theories, so the Buddha, speaking to lay people and not to philosophers, would have used these words quite informally.

42   I was recently surprised to find a description of investigations which fall strikingly into line with the Buddha's teaching: "the ability of the lower brainstem to discriminate between sensory signals and 'decide' that some events are welcome while others must be rejected as unpleasant or harmful. People are inclined to believe that discrimination between good and bad is a cognitive function base on life experience, learning, habit and an emotional attitude. This is not so." (Richard E. Cytowic, "The Man Who Tasted Shapes", Putnam, New York(1993)). Cytowic went on to describe certain experiments in self-awareness: "The illusive nature of self-awareness was first shown by Kornhuber in 1965. His work on what is called the 'readiness potential' shows that there is more to conscious-ness than what is apparent from either what we can introspect or observe. The experimental subject is told to move a finger whenever he or she feels like it. Devices measure precisely when finger movement occurs as well as electrical potentials in the brain before and after the movement. A spe-cial clock permits the subject to record the moment of conscious decision to move the finger...one finds a buildup of brain activity, the readiness potential, that prepares the action to be performed. This occurs in the brain about one second before the subject makes a conscious decision to move the finger...In other words, the readiness potential far antedates the subject's decision to make a movement... The conclusion is that we are deluded in believing that each of us is a free agent who may decide to take an action. Such a decision is an interpretation we give to a behaviour that has been initiated some place else by another part of ourselves well before we are aware of making a decision at all. In other words, the deci-

sion has been made before we are aware of the idea to even make a decision. If 'we' are not pulling the strings, then who or what is?"

43   *Udāna*.8

44   I recently came across a quotation by Ma Tsu of Kiangsi: 'Your own
treasure house contains everything you need. Use it freely instead of
searching vainly for something outside yourself.'

45   *Milinda-Pañha*, chapter 3

46   *Saṁyutta Nikāya*, I, 135
47   BUDDHADASA BHIKKHU, "Buddhism Now", IV no.4 (Nov'94), p. 3.

48   *Majjhima Nikāya, sutta* 26. This passage occurs in two other places in
the Canon. The occasion was after the Buddha's enlightenment when he
despaired at the apparent impossibility of ever putting the essence of the
Dhamma across to the people. It was the timely appearance of Brahma
Sahampati who spoke of the needs of those "with little dust in their eyes"
that persuaded the Buddha to devote himself to teaching for the rest of
his life.

49   See for example E.Conze's "Buddhist Wisdom Books: The Heart
Sutra", p.3. The "Buddhist Wisdom Books" (*Prajñāpāramitā*) are not part of
the Pali Canon, but are the most important scriptures of the Mahayana
teaching.

50   ROGER PENROSE, "The Emperor's New Mind".

51   SRI NISARGADATTA MAHARAJ, "I am That", Part 1, Chetana, Bombay
(1973), p.62.

52   CHUANG TSU, "The Inner Chapters", translated by Gia Fu Feng and Jane English, Wild Wood House, London (1974), Chapter 2.

53   OLIVER SACKS, "An Anthropologist on Mars", (Picador, 1995) p. 53, footnote 7.

54   *Majjhima Nikāya, Sutta* 38 ("Middle Length Sayings", I, p. 321.)

55   KRISHNAMURTI, "Notebook", Gollancz paperback (1985), p.51
56   MOTHER MEERA, "Answers", Rider paperback (1991), p.78

INDEX

A

Abhidhamma Pitaka   113
Abu Sa'id   103
Achaan Cha   118
against the stream   29, 83
aggregates, five   13
aim in meditation   102
akusala   54, 106
anapanasati   110
anatta   18, 41, 61, 86, 106
  (see also self)
animal welfare   46
Arahant (Perfected One)   13, 69, 106
arrow, poisoned   20, 84
Asanga   33
Asoka, King   20
astrology   79-82
  charts   79
astronomy   32
atheist   84
atman,atta   19, 28
  (see also self)
atoms   88
avijja   54, 106
awakening   21, 51
awareness (see also sati)   9

B

belief   17, 83-86
  Sati's mistaken belief   23, 26
  (see also doctrine, ditthi)
  and scientists   40
Bharadvaja   63, 64

bhava   53,68,106
bhavana   74, 83, 106
bhavanga   74, 106
bhunahuno   69
black holes   35, 84
blind man   67, 68
blind men and elephant   39
Blofeld   21
body
  body/mind   57
  impurities   11
  not me, not mine   29
  watching   10, 11
Boyle, Robert   6
Brahma   53, 84
Brahma, Day & Night of   38
brahma-farer   68
brahma-viharas   109
brahmins   18
brain
  activity   120
  hierarchy   57
  & nervous system   57
Buddha
  advice to the Kalamas   15, 16
  Age-old message   17
  against the stream   29, 83
  arrow,poisoned   20, 84
  bundles of reeds   29
  energy   50
  honey-cake   53-62
  know-for-yourselves   101
  Magandiya   63-71
  raft   19

sati 23-30
Satipatthana 9-13
Sutta Nipata 27
Vachagotta 19, 28
worldlings 95
blind man 71
burning with attachment 66, 70
butterfly dream 99

C

California Personality
  Inventory(CPI) 80
car, learning to drive 58
Carlson,Shawn 79
caste system 18
central perception 61
chariot 39
Chalmers 69
charnel-house contemplation 11, 116
Childers dictionary 7, 69, 74
Chinese invasion of Tibet 21
Christian countries 84
Chuang Tzu 99
Citta 10, 107, 116
Citta, watching 12
clairvoyants 82
clinging 11, 21, 25
compassion 45
computers 38, 74
continental drift 84
Consciousness 23-30, 73-78
  (see also vinnana)
  arising 24,75
  discontinuous 61
  eye-,-ear, etc. 24, 75
  like fire 25
  name-and-form 29, 107
  open 74
  other 74
  self 74

contemplative life 45
control systems 57
CPI 80
craving, destruction of 25
Curie, Mme 89
cynicism 6, 40

D

Dalai Lama 47
Dalton's atomic theory 33
death, dead bodies 11
deities 21
Democritus 33
destroyer of well-being 64
devas 53, 65, 107
deva world 65, 107
development, spiritual 69
Devil 105, 117
Dhamma 68, 69, 107
  activity 49
  images of the mind 10
  raft 19
  Sati the Fisherman 23-30
  science 31-42
  social action 45
  swimming in 7
  watching 12
Digha Nikaya 5, 108, 111, 113
disarmament, nuclear 46
ditthi 26, 54
doctrine, doctrinal 17, 26, 41
  (see also belief)
Dogen 44
dream 95-99
dukkha 55, 61, 68, 108
  & 3 signs of being 26
  ending of 85

E

Eightfold Path   26, 67, 71
Einstein   39, 87
electrons   88
electromagnetic   89
elementary particles   35
elements, four   11
enlightenment
  seven factors   13
emergent properties   74
emptiness and form   87-90
ending of dukkha   85
energy
  & activity   50
  kinetic   36
evil   88
Eysenck   81
exploring   41

F

feedback   74
feelings, watching   11
fever of the mind   66, 102
fire   27, 66, 70, 75
Fire Sermon   27, 75
five hindrances   12
five aggregates   13
flame analogy   76

form and emptiness   87-90
formative causation   33
four forces:
  gravity, electromagnetism,
  strong and weak   89
Four Foundations of awareness 9,13
Four Noble Truths   26
freedom   19
Freud   69

G

Gauquelin   81
genes   33
  not "me"   76
God, gods   19,84,103
  God's creation   88
Graham, Aelred   104
Gravity, Law of   32
groups, Buddhist   45

H

Hawkin, Stephen   87
health   66,71
Heart Sutra   90
Heisenberg, Werner   35
hindrances, five   12
hierarchical systems   58
Hiroshima   38
homeless   65
honey-cake   53-62
humans and animals   39
Huxley, Aldous   101
hypothesis   32, 35

I

I   47, 60
  (see also self)
  the watcher   97
illness   65
illusion   29,46
images   21
impurities   11
individuality   78
indriya   108
interdependent origination   23, 27
intolerance, scientific   85
introvert   45
involvement   43-47

inwardly calm   66
Israel, Martin   103

J

Jesus, turning the other cheek   92
Jeta Grove   23
jewels, museum of   73
jhana   105
jhanic states   111
Jones, Ken   44
judgement   85
Jung   47

K

Kaccano the Great   54, 55
Kalamas   15-16, 40
kalpa, kappa   17, 38, 118
kamma,karma   18, 86, 91-94, 108
  kamma vipaka(fruits of kamma)
108,112
karma buck   91-94
karuna   109
kaya   10, 108, 110,
khandhas   60, 109, 110
Khantipalo   8, 16
Krishnamurti   99, 104
kurus   9
kusala   109

L

laser   35
Leggett, Trevor   82
leper,leprosy   65, 66, 70
light   36
little dust in their eyes   20, 121
love   21, 45

M

Magandiya   63-71
Majjhima Nikaya   84, 95, 112, 113
man, of old   71
mano   54
Mara the Tempter   39
materialism   32, 66
mathematics   35
matter and space   88
me, mine   96
  (see also self)
meditation (see also sati)   102
Mencken's Law   43
mental models   35, 37
Meera, Mother   105
message, age-old   17
metta   109
Middle Way   44
Mindfulness   7
  the still mind   30
  (see also sati)
miracles   118
mudita   98, 109
Mulapariyaya sutta   95
Muslim countries   84
mystery   21, 47
mystics
  Christian & Muslim   84

N

namarupa(name-and-form)   29-30,
  109
National Council for Geocosmic
Research   80
Neumann, John Von   36, 88
neutrinos   89
Newton   32
Nibbana, Nirvana   5, 9, 66, 67, 106,
  109

Nibbana as ending of fever   71
Nisargadatta   19, 94, 104
non-violence   93
nucleus,atomic   88
Nyananda, Bhikkhu   55,110
Nyanaponika Mahathera   6
nuclear disarmament   46

O

Occam's razor   34
occult power   44
omens   85
ordinary uninstructed worldling   61
ordination   68

P

palaces, three   65
Pali Canon   7, 113
palmistry   82
panna   108
papanca &
  papanca-sanna-sankha   53-56, 60,
  62, 110
paradigm   40
Parkinson' disease   57
particles and waves   36
paticca samuppada
  (interdependent origination,
  conditioned genesis)   23, 27, 110
perception   11
perennial philosophy &
  practice   101
person, chariot   39, 77
personality profile   80
phasso   54-57, 110
philosophical opinion   25, 120
  sense   29
physics   30
pigeon holes   82

planetary influence   82
pleasant/unpleasant   59
poisoned arrow   20, 84
politics   46
practice   101
Prajnaparamita   87
prejudices   85
protein   33
psychic powers   16, 32
'psychic genes'   76
Pyrro the Sceptic   40

Q

quarks   88

R

raft   19
Rahula, Walpola Sri   107
Ramana Maharshi   17
religion
  and science   31-41
rebirth and kamma/karma   18, 23, 75,
  76
repressive   64
Rhys Davies dict.   7
rights, a person's   93
robe,greasy   71
robots   39
rupa   68, 109, 110
Russell, Bertrand   36, 88

S

saddha   108
samadhi   108, 110
samatha   112
samma ditthi   26, 111
samsara   106, 110, 111
Sangha   19, 111
sanjanati   56, 57, 110

sankharas   111
sanna   109, 111, 119
sati   44, 50, 51, 93, 108
Satipatthana   7, 21, 97, 102
Sati the Fisherman's Son   23-30, 75
scepticism   5, 40, 85
science & Buddhism   31-41
sects   45
see for themselves   16, 18
self (see also anatta,I,me)
  annihilation of   29
  Dogen   44
  fulfilment   86
  not my body   96
sense organs,six   13
  guarded & controlled   64
serenity   86
Seven Factors of Enlightenment   13
shark   57
Sheldrake, Rupert   33, 77
simplicity   81
sixth sense   16
sleep   28
social action   44
Solar System   38
  solar influence   63
space and time   37
  and matter   88
spending time   49
spectrum of attitudes   44
spiritual experience   75
still mind   21
subconscious   69, 74
supernatural   14, 23
suffering and the end of,   20, 21, 90
Sutta Nipata   26, 83, 98
Suzuki, Shunryu   103

T

Tao The Ching   84
teaching, perennial   17
Theravada suttas   25, 112
thirst (tanha)   40, 112
Tibet   21
transmigration & rebirth   76
Truman, President   91
TV set   34, 77

U

unconscious   73, 74
upadana   110
upekha   109
Ussher, Bishop   38

V

Vachagotta   19, 28
Vajira, Nun   39
vedana   54-59, 68, 77, 109, 110, 112
Vedanta, Vedas   19, 104
views,right   111
Vinaya   69, 77
vinnana   54, 56, 68, 77, 109, 112
vipaka   88
vipassana   112, 117
viriya   108
vitakka   54, 62
Von Neumann   36, 88

W

Walshe,Maurice   7, 110
watcher, I the   97
watching
  the body (kaya)   10
  the feelings(vedana)   11
  citta   12
  Dhamma   12

waves of the sea   46-47
Wei Wu Wei   99
witchcraft   85
wood-turner   10
world, external & internal   96
  many worlds   90
worldling   96
worship   20
Wright, Wilbur   58

Z

zodiac   82
Zen Mind, Beginner's Mind   103
Zen monks   30